A Measure of Malpractice

A Measure of Malpractice

Medical Injury,
Malpractice Litigation,
and Patient Compensation

PAUL C. WEILER

HOWARD H. HIATT

JOSEPH P. NEWHOUSE

WILLIAM G. JOHNSON

TROYEN A. BRENNAN

LUCIAN L. LEAPE

HARVARD UNIVERSITY PRESS
Cambridge, Massachusetts
London, England   1993

Library of Congress Cataloging-in-Publication Data

Measure of malpractice : medical injury, malpractice litigation, and
   patient compensation / Paul C. Weiler . . . [et al.].
      p.   cm.
   Includes index.
   ISBN 0-674-55880-4 (alk. paper)
   1. Physicians—Malpractice—United States. 2. Insurance,
Physicians' liability—United States. 3. Malpractice—Economic
aspects—Research—United States. I. Weiler, Paul C.
   [DNLM: 1. Insurance, Liability. 2. Liability, Legal.
3. Malpractice—New York. 4. Wounds and Injuries—epidemiology—New
York.   44 M484]
KF2905.3.M4 1993
346.7303'32—dc20
[347.306332]
DNLM/DLC
for Library of Congress   92-1705
                                                                      CIP

Contents

Preface

The complexities of many problems facing contemporary society respect neither the disciplinary lines that separate professions nor those that distinguish the several faculties of today's university. A vivid example is the interplay of the legal and the health care systems as the two grapple with the problems of physician error and patient injury in medical care. In 1984 the mounting personal and economic costs of this problem led then Deans Howard Hiatt of the Harvard School of Public Health and James Vorenberg of the Harvard Law School to invite several of their colleagues to form the Harvard Medical Practice Study Group to undertake interdisciplinary analysis of this problem area. At that time, as now, there was mutual recognition that neither law nor medicine had yet devised satisfactory approaches to this problem. But agreement ended at the point when the participants began discussing what would constitute effective and fitting remedies for these deficiencies.

For well over a year the original members of the Study Group debated the standard array of proposals for malpractice reform. The doctors were principally interested in caps on damage awards and alternatives to trial by jury, which together would offer health care providers some relief from an erratic and burdensome litigation system. The lawyers sought ways of making tort law even more accessible to seriously injured patients who needed redress, and of imposing stiffer sanctions on doctors whose negligence had caused injury to their patients.

As the membership of the group gradually changed, it dawned on us that we were mired in these controversies because we suffered from the same information gap that was afflicting legislators and courts asked to choose from this policy menu. The case for these proposals rested almost entirely on anecdotal evidence, too easily tailored to the predispositions of the protagonist. A growing body of serious research instructed lawmakers that if they adopted one kind of measure as opposed to another, a real difference would result in the number of malpractice suits filed and the size of damage awards rendered. But with the conspicuous exception of a pathbreaking study of the incidence of medical injury in California in the mid-1970s, there was nothing that would permit governments or citizens to make informed judgments about whether it was a good idea to reduce—or, alternatively, increase—the rate of malpractice litigation.

Eventually we concluded that as scholars in a university, our responsibility and our comparative advantage lay in doing the kind of research that could fill this yawning gap in the malpractice debate. Accordingly, we mapped out an ambitious study that for the first time would come to grips with all the major facets of this problem: the nature and extent of medical injury, the losses inflicted on patients and the redress secured from non-tort sources, the extent to which patients who had been negligently injured (and those who had not) had recourse to malpractice litigation, and the impact of the tort system on physician behavior and patient injury. Only after immersing ourselves in this process of empirical discovery and analysis would we be in a position to offer our views about how to improve the law's treatment of medical care. And such a research program promised a potentially more important side benefit: it could provide a range of valuable insights for those working in the nascent quality assurance field within health care itself.

We then took this carefully designed research program to the key officials in both government and organized medicine in our home state of Massachusetts, seeking access to hospitals and doctors as well as financial support for the project. We were surprised at the rather cool response that we received from both quarters. Further investigation, however, revealed the reason. A bill was then pending in the state legislature, supported by both the administration and the medical society, that proposed to enact versions of the standard malpractice reform proposals (including a cap on pain and suffering awards and a stiffer medical disciplinary regime). No one wanted to jeopardize enactment of these controversial solutions by having legislators learn that a comprehensive study was being undertaken on the nature of the problem.

Happily for us, just when our project seemed becalmed, we encountered Dr. David Axelrod, the Commissioner of Health of New York and the central figure in the efforts of the Cuomo administration to grapple with these very issues in that state. Dr. Axelrod needed no persuasion of the value of this kind of research. With his support, the governor and the legislature attached to their pending malpractice reform bill a provision that would require and fund a systematic empirical study to help shape the future course of action in the state. Our diffidence about presenting our cost estimate of $4 million for the three-year Harvard Study was allayed by Dr. Axelrod's observation that New York doctors and hospitals—and through them, New York citizens—were well on their way to spending $1 *billion* annually for malpractice insurance.

While there were obvious logistical difficulties inherent in a Harvard-based group's carrying out such research in New York, that state also offered critical advantages. New York is large and diverse in its population and patients, in its economic and social programs, in the kind and quality of its health care providers, and in the extent to which its malpractice system was being used by patients and directed at doctors. Consequently, gathering and analyzing data from this rich and varied experience promised us both statistically significant results within the state and findings that would be highly relevant to the malpractice debate across the nation.

But the most important resource that New York offered us was David Axelrod. Dr. Axelrod won the support of the New York State Medical Society and eventually of the American Medical Association. He secured for us the cooperation of a host of people in the Department of Health, the Department of Insurance, and, most important, in the state's hospitals. In addition, he regularly provided us with illuminating suggestions about the focus and design of our research. We cannot overstate the vital role played in the Harvard Study by David Axelrod, as in so many of his other major initiatives that will contribute enormously to the health of Americans.

The support of Dr. Axelrod and his colleagues in the Department of Health was indispensable as we grappled with the inevitable differences between mapping an ambitious research program on paper and actually implementing it. We proposed to discover and describe how many patients were injured in New York hospitals and how many of these injuries were the result of someone's negligence; how many of these patients then brought suits, and whether the suits actually filed were those that should have been filed; how extensive were the financial losses suffered by injured patients and how generous were alternative sources of compensation; and what impact the experience of being sued had on the doctors' own behavior and on the risk of injury to patients. Searching for the answers to these questions required that we gather and analyze huge masses of information. We eventually sifted through 30,000 hospital records, tracked down and interviewed 2,500 patients, surveyed 1,000 doctors, and examined data from the nearly 70,000 malpractice claims filed in New York from 1975 into 1989. To obtain the needed information, we had to have access to hospitals and their records, to examine litigation data that liability insurers and self-insured hospitals were supposed to provide the state government, to locate and interview injured patients about their subsequent experience, and to survey physicians who had experienced or observed the consequences of being sued. All of this work had to be conducted in conformity with our assurances of strict confidentiality. The following examples of problems we confronted and dealt with should provide some indication of the nature and complexity of the task and explain why the project stretched on for six years before we were able to offer our conclusions in this book.

As we will detail in Chapter 3, our study of the extent of medical injury was based on in-depth analysis of the hospital records of patients. Crucial to the design of this study was selection of a representative sample of patients from a group of hospitals that was large enough to give a fair picture of the diversity among patients, doctors, and lawyers in the state, but small enough that we could reasonably manage locating and moving our operation from one hospital to the next. Eventually we selected 51 hospitals, roughly 20 percent of the state's acute-care nonpsychiatric facilities. It was vital for us to gain access to and cooperation from all but a handful of these hospitals, so that findings from our sample would be statistically representative. To the outside viewer, at least, refusal by any one institution to participate in such a study might not be just a random event, but rather evidence of a special problem that particular hospital wanted to conceal.

On the other hand, consent was not automatically forthcoming from all the hospitals. For one thing, the study placed an immediate burden on the staff of each facility that was asked to locate and organize hundreds of files, many of which were regularly moving in and out of the hospital's record room for purposes of patient care. Indeed, when the study eventually did get under way, we were astonished and gratified by the near total retrieval success that was accomplished by hospital personnel.

That logistical burden alone was one that hospital administrators would probably have accepted, given their recognition that better scientific understanding of the malpractice problem was essential for satisfactory solutions to the liability crisis they themselves were experiencing. The administrators were far more concerned about the specific liability risk posed by the study itself.

In today's legal climate, it is understandable that health care providers worry about investigations that might well uncover information which could be used in a lawsuit. Even worse, our research agenda involved not simply determining from written records whether a patient had been negligently injured in treatment, but also locating and interviewing patients about their experience following hospitalization. We had deliberately selected 1984 as the hospital treatment year because it fell beyond the two-and-a-half-year statutory limitation period for malpractice claims. However, hospitals and their lawyers were pardonably skeptical that this protection was legally airtight. It was a year before our efforts, along with those of Dr. Axelrod, the Health Department, and the state Hospital Association, persuaded all the hospitals and their staffs that the study design contained sufficient safeguards of confidentiality and protection against liability. (The fifty-first hospital had a change of leadership after the other 50 had signed up. Happily for us, the new president, who had been a student of one of us and was sympathetic to our goals, persuaded his colleagues to participate.)

One of the confidentiality guarantees itself raised a problem in our dealing with patients. As we shall see in subsequent chapters, inter-

viewing patients regarding the financial consequences of initial medical injuries was a crucial component of our overall research program. It was difficult enough to locate 3,000 patients five years after
they had been admitted to a hospital: many had moved several times
since then, and several of these now had no known address or
telephone number. Having eventually located 90 percent of our sample, however, we then had to persuade the patients or their surviving
dependents to undergo an interview of an hour or more that entailed
detailed recollection of much that had happened in their lives since
they left the hospital. After considerable experience and follow-up
efforts, Mathematica Policy Research of Princeton, New Jersey, eventually persuaded 90 percent of the located and eligible patients to
participate.

All the interviews had to be conducted in accordance with our
commitment to the hospitals that no mention at all would be made
of the fact that any patient had been injured in the hospital, let alone
as the result of a doctor's negligence. Interviewers could ask no
questions about whether the patient had brought suit, nor even
comment that the study was related to the malpractice liability debate. The subjects to be interviewed, comprising both medically injured patients and a matched control group of patients who had not
been injured during treatment, were informed twice—in a letter from
Dr. Axelrod, and in their contacts with Mathematica—that the study
was about "the economic consequences of hospitalization." Indeed,
the interviewers themselves were unaware that any of their patient-
subjects had been injured and that the study was at all related to the
issue of malpractice.

This adherence to the commitments we made to the hospitals
obviously raised ethical questions about the patients' interest in full
disclosure. If we had told the interviewees everything we knew, they
would have learned about both the general nature of the investigation and their own medical history. On the other hand, if we had
told the hospitals that we were prepared to give the patients this
information, we would not have had access to any of the hospitals,
the medical records would not have been available for analysis, and
there would thus have been no information to convey to the
patient—indeed, there would have been no basis for identifying and
setting out to interview any patients injured during treatment. Nor,

needless to say, would there have been any way to gather and analyze the broader data from this study to permit more informed debate about improving the medical liability system for future patients. However, we held extensive discussions on this issue with Professor William Curran of the Harvard School of Public Health and the members of the Human Subjects Committee, which he then chaired. Eventually the project design was approved by the committees. At that point we decided that in good conscience we could comply with the confidentiality commitments we had made to the hospitals and their medical staffs.

This study required the participation of scholars from a variety of disciplines and perspectives—not only medicine and law, but also economics, statistics, survey research, and data management. The authors of this book are the people who have been centrally involved in the project. At the start we were agreed only that the malpractice debate could benefit from more informed analysis and less fervent conviction. Most of the following chapters are devoted to an account of what information we were looking for and why, how we assembled the data, what we discovered, and what our findings imply for the broader policy debate. After six years of immersion in the design, execution, and analysis of this daunting empirical study, we were happy to discover that our personal views had begun to converge on common policy ground. The final chapter presents our joint reflections about promising avenues for improving the treatment of patient injuries in both the legal and the health care systems.

Several people played crucial roles in planning, carrying out, and analyzing the results of the Harvard Medical Practice Study. Nan Laird, Professor of Biostatistics at the Harvard School of Public Health, directed the randomization process and was key in interpreting the hospital records study. Dr. Benjamin Barnes played an important role in planning and developing the hospital records study. Russell Localio, a lawyer-statistician, managed several aspects of the project, helped design the hospital records study, and directed the collection and analysis of the claims data. Ann Lawthers, a health policy analyst, was initially administrative director of the study and later coordinator and designer of the provider studies. William Hsiao, Professor of Economics at the Harvard School of Public Health, helped in the planning phase. Ken Thorpe, an economist at the School of Public Health, and Carl Morris, Professor of Statistics and Professor of Health Care Policy in the Faculty of Medicine at Harvard, made important contributions to the deterrence studies. Doctors Sol Fleischman, Howard Frazier, and Lynn Peterson served as senior physician reviewers for the hospital records review portion of the study. Helen Burstin, Liesi Hebert, and Stuart Lipsitz participated in the analysis of the hospital record data.

Consultants to the project included Floyd J. Fowler, Jr., Director of the Center for Survey Research, University of Massachusetts; Graham Kalton, Chairman of the Department of Biostatistics at the University of Michigan; Ruth Kilduff, Risk Manager at New England Medical Center; Donald Rubin, head of the Department of Statistics at Harvard University; and Alan Zaslavsky, Lecturer in Statistics at Harvard.

Valuable assistance in administration, computation, and data management was provided by Sybil Carey, Elaine Gebhardt, Steven Marcus, Alison Eastwood, Chris Braudaway-Bauman, Wendy Vander Hart, Sandra Lee Gould, Robert Chaufornier, and Marilyn Martino.

Special thanks are owed to Sylvia Baldwin, who typed and corrected numerous versions of the manuscript; and to Florrie Darwin, who edited, proofread, and prepared the index for the book.

Our early work was supported by a Klingenstein Fund grant that permitted us to explore the terrain and to make an informed decision whether to proceed. Once that decision was made, Dan Creasey, President of the Risk Management Foundation, made it possible for us to do so. The major part of our work was supported by the State of New York with funds from the legislature and from the Department of Health. Finally, completion of our analyses and examination of their policy implications were made possible by grants from the Robert Wood Johnson Foundation.

We are grateful to all these parties for their help in making this study and this book possible.

CHAPTER 1

The Malpractice Setting

The Harvard Medical Practice Study was commissioned in 1986 by the state of New York as part of a major legislative reform of its medical liability laws. At that time a sense of crisis enveloped the malpractice system as premiums were skyrocketing in New York and across the nation. In that atmosphere Section 39 of the state's new Medical and Dental Malpractice and Professional Conduct Act directed that a study be done of the "extent of medical and dental injury regardless of fault, the extent to which such injuries are compensated by sources of compensation outside the liability system, and an analysis of alternative insurance or liability mechanisms . . . including the feasibility of medical compensation systems that could compensate victims irrespective of fault."

The mood is very different today, as we systematically draw together here all the key findings of the empirical investigation we undertook pursuant to that mandate. Beginning in 1989 the malpractice price spiral first slowed and then plateaued: premiums now have dropped somewhat from their peak levels.[1] The temperature level in the malpractice debate has also dropped considerably, generating less political urgency even to revise the existing system, let alone to contemplate fundamental alternatives.

Close observers of the malpractice regime are not so sanguine, however. They realize that the trend in insurance premiums constitutes a rather ambiguous symptom of the ailments that may be afflicting the interplay of our medical and legal systems. Equally important, those who have lived through the sharply cyclical pattern of malpractice insurance price jumps and pauses over the last several decades appreciate that yet another sizable premium increase may be lurking just around the corner in the mid-1990s.

Recognizing these facts, the American Medical Association continues to press its proposal for an "administrative fault" system[2] in certain states, including Vermont and Utah. The American Law Institute recently released its study on tort liability and tort reform,[3] calling for profound changes in the legal treatment of medical injury. In the spring of 1991 President Bush delivered to the Congress a message that seeks to use the federal government's Medicaid-financing lever to prod the states to enact his administration's favored tort reforms. And in New York State itself Governor Cuomo, building on earlier initiatives in Virginia and Florida, has proposed enactment of a broad no-fault "Compensation Program for the Impaired Newborn" to replace much of existing obstetrical liability.

Trends in Malpractice Premiums and Litigation

One obvious reason for these enduring concerns about the malpractice system is that even if premiums seem for the moment to have reached a plateau, the height of that plateau appears astonishing to the casual onlooker. In New York State, for example, the average doctor paid $360 (in 1990 dollars) for liability coverage in 1949.[4] Sixteen years later, in 1965, the cost of such coverage was just $1,000, but it then leaped to $7,300 by 1975. And by the end of the 1980s the average cost of reasonably full insurance protection for doctors (against claims of up to $3 million each) was near $40,000 —more than 100 times the price of the same protection four decades earlier. In the higher-risk specialties and regions, such as neurosurgery, orthopedic surgery, and obstetrics in places like New York City and Long Island, the premium cost to provide $3 million of coverage to a single doctor (which is not even full protection against a potential jury award in the most severe cases) ranges from $150,000 to $200,000 a year.

New York's malpractice premium levels, while among the highest in the country, are not unique. Doctors in states such as Florida, Michigan, and Illinois face comparable charges. And even in the states where insurance costs are at or near the national average—

roughly $15,000 a year per physician—the path that premium rates have followed to that level has been similar to the rise in rates in New York and equally troubling.

Medical liability costs began to rise sharply in the late 1960s, leading the Nixon administration to appoint a national commission to analyze the problem. The commission's report, issued in 1973, was decidedly nonalarmist in tone. Its basic verdict was that doctors did not need special legal protection not afforded to other tort defendants. But the ink was barely dry on the commission's report when the country's first malpractice "crisis" emerged in the mid-1970s, with premium levels doubling in just three years. Numerous states, including New York, responded with legislation that favored doctors with a variety of measures in malpractice litigation. In the immediate aftermath of this legislative effort the malpractice insurance market stabilized, with real premiums increasing quite slowly for the next several years. Unfortunately that equilibrium did not hold. A second equally severe malpractice crisis occurred in the mid-1980s, with premium levels again doubling in just three years. State legislatures were galvanized into action once more, with many states this time giving other tort defendants the benefit of the favorable measures they were devising for doctors.

Whatever the causes of the overall increases in malpractice premiums or the merits of the legislative responses, the premium pattern just described produces an understandable sense of grievance among doctors. The individual physician needs to have liability insurance in order to be able to practice with a reasonable degree of financial security. However, even if the doctor has never been sued, let alone been found liable, he or she faces sudden steep hikes in this major item in the cost of practice, price hikes for which it is difficult to adjust immediately the fees charged for the doctor's services (especially in the face of recent cost containment efforts by public and private health insurers). In addition, given this cyclical pattern of jumps and pauses in malpractice premiums, it is understandable that physicians and their professional associations do not draw great comfort from the current premium stability.

It seems reasonably clear that the highly erratic path followed by malpractice premiums is primarily attributable to the special characteristics of liability insurance and the insurance industry. However, the long-term trend in the price of malpractice insurance is the result of the steadily rising cost of the doctor's liability itself.

The cost of legal liability is a function of the number of claims filed against health care providers (claims frequency) and the average payment made on successful claims (claims severity). Though there is on this issue no single body of consistent data extending across the last several decades, there is no mistaking the picture that emerges from various data sources available at different points of time. Claims frequency, measured by the number of claims per doctor per year, rose from just over 1 claim per 100 doctors per year in the late 1950s to well over 10 claims per 100 doctors in the mid-1980s before settling back somewhat by the end of the 1980s. At the same time, the average payment made on successful claims rose from $40,000 (in 1990 dollars) in 1970 to nearly $150,000 by the end of the 1980s. In retrospect the remarkable jump in malpractice premiums in the middle of this decade appears to represent insurers' overreacting to what they feared was happening in the legal system. However, the fact that premium levels have declined only modestly from their 1988 peak shows that the steep increases in prices charged in the insurance market do reflect the cumulative rise in legal liability costs incurred by the health care system.[5]

And one can understand, if not justify, the insurers' overreaction to what they perceived to be happening in the legal system. Liability insurance is a difficult product to price because roughly two-thirds of its costs of production (the payments ultimately made on tort claims) are incurred sometime after the year in which the product is first sold. That percentage is even higher in the case of medical liability, which has a much longer "tail" than does motor vehicle liability, for example, between the original injury and a malpractice claim, as well as between the filing and the disposition of a claim. The inability of malpractice insurers to detect and guard against an upward trend in liability cost was vividly depicted in a study done by the Superintendent of Insurance in New York State.[6] This study compared the New York insurers' income—money received in premiums plus investment returns on premium reserves—against insurer outlays—payments to claimants and administrative/legal expenses—for each treatment year covered by the insurers from 1959 through 1979. The study found that for each of the years in that twenty-year period, insurer actuaries had been unduly optimistic in projecting future liability costs. As a consequence, the carriers, in effect, had to "borrow" money from premiums paid in later years to cover the shortfall in revenues needed to pay liability costs incurred for earlier years.

The legal system, then, does impose a real cost burden on malpractice insurance. An additional factor seriously aggravating the threat of liability faced by health care providers is the huge award that may unpredictably be rendered in any single case. Medical malpractice annually produces one of the two or three largest jury awards in the entire American legal system: a $52 million malpractice verdict in Houston in 1988, a $54 million verdict in Los Angeles in 1989, a $78 million award in Chicago in 1990, and a stunning $127 million award against an Illinois ophthalmologist in 1991. One should be under no illusion, though, that inordinately generous sums of money are being won by the typical patient-victim of medical negligence.

First of all, after the time of injury a lengthy period transpires before the patient receives any legal relief at all. In the nation as a whole, the *median* time from injury to claim is 13 months, and from claim to payment 23 months, for a total of three years. The most serious injuries, those generating the greatest financial needs for patients, take considerably longer to resolve. For example, in New York the *average* delay between initial injury and eventual payment is six years—often a decade or more for the most severe injuries. And since many states still do not pay prejudgment interest on their awards, health care providers benefit and patients lose as a result of these inevitable delays in the operation of the legal system.

Even after waiting so long, only about half of those patients who file claims ultimately receive any payment. Partly because of the delay factor just mentioned, the most severely injured victims—those with the greatest needs for immediate relief—settle their claims for the smallest proportion of their actual losses. Moreover, roughly one-third of the money received by the patient-victim from the malpractice insurer is paid to the patient's lawyer under the standard percentage contingent fee arrangement, which gives the lawyer nothing if the claim fails. (About 60 percent of patients who use lawyers do receive some settlement or award.)

Most important of all, our study (see Chapter 4) found that only a small fraction of patients with potentially valid tort claims—that is, patients who suffer a disabling injury caused by the negligence of some health care provider—ever file a malpractice claim in the first place, let alone succeed in collecting any money after the law's lengthy delays. So the steady increase in claims frequency and severity we noted earlier reflects merely a partial closing of the large gap between potential and actual malpractice claims, not an inordinate level of litigation inflicted by the law on the medical system.

At the same time, one should not assume that these patient injuries and claims are the work of just a handful of particularly accident-prone doctors—so-called bad apples. For example, an analysis by the New York Department of Health[7] of claims closed against that state's doctors from 1980 through 1983 found that only 131 doctors—just 0.36 percent of the state's 35,552 practicing physicians—had been the target of more than two paid tort claims, and most of these doctors were found in the inherently higher-risk specialties of surgery and obstetrics. In any event, even these more suit-prone doctors produced only a small fraction (less than 10 percent) of the total of paid claims in New York. Moreover, a later Florida study[8] indicates that membership in this target group changes considerably from one four-year period to the next. As later chapters of this book will document, modern medicine is an inherently risky enterprise. Momentary inadvertent mistakes can be made by even the most careful and concerned doctors, just as such mistakes are made by doctors' professional counterparts in other fields such as law or insurance. But unlike the error of a litigator or actuary, the slip-up of a surgeon in a delicate operation may result in severe and irreversible physical injury to a patient. The by-products of the inevitable human mistakes and injuries in medical practice are tort suits whose costs are ultimately borne by the malpractice insurance system, giving rise to premium levels that have soared for the last quarter-century.

Legislative Responses to Malpractice Crises

The sense of crisis that recurrently overtakes the malpractice system is, not surprisingly, also felt by state politicians. In New York and elsewhere in the country, significant legislative changes have been enacted in an effort to alleviate the problems felt by doctors with malpractice litigation. Waves of such legislative activity occurred initially in 1975–76 and then again in 1985–86, coinciding with the peak points in the premium spiral.[9]

These statutory changes addressed numerous facets of each of the three distinct components of the overall malpractice regime. One component is the liability insurance system, which has generated the sharply increased premium bills to hospitals and doctors needed to cover the large liability costs incurred by providers to their patients. The second component is the tort litigation process, which determines which injured patients will be able to collect on their tort claims and how much compensation successful claimants will receive. The third major component is the health care system itself, in which patients are looked after by doctors and other providers, and in which the treatment occasionally exacerbates rather than ameliorates the patient's condition, consequently moving some patients to seek legal and monetary relief. Without going into detail, it will be useful simply to mention the key reform measures that have been introduced in New York and many other states.

LIABILITY INSURANCE

- To fill the vacuum left by the withdrawal of any commercial insurance from the rather unstable malpractice market, new provider-controlled carriers—"bedpan mutuals," as they are colloquially called—were formed in most states. In addition, a few states mandated the creation of joint underwriting associations comprising all carriers doing business in the state, to serve as a last-resort guarantee to practicing physicians against having to "go bare" of any insurance protection.
- Malpractice insurers were authorized to write and offer "claims made" rather than "occurrence" policies. This new type of insurance provided coverage for claims made during the year for which the policy was written rather than for the earlier year during which treatment was given and the injury occurred. These new policies thus enabled insurers to price their coverage for a time frame that was somewhat closer to the point of possible payment of a claim.

- Individual doctors have been relieved of some of their personal responsibility to pay for the patient's injuries, either by a requirement that the hospital where the treatment took place "channel" such liability through the institution's insurance policy, or by the creation of a patient compensation fund sustained by all providers in the state (or even perhaps by the state's taxpayers).
- New York and Massachusetts have mandated merit rating of malpractice insurance, so that those doctors who have experienced abnormally high rates of claims or payments in the past will be charged somewhat higher premiums for this insurance coverage in the future.

MALPRACTICE LITIGATION

Statutory reform of the tort litigation system was directed at each of its three key points: accessibility to claimants, determination of provider liability, and assessment of damages payable.

- Measures to contain the entry of claims into the litigation process included somewhat shorter statutes of limitation and the addition of statutes of repose, mandatory certification, or review panel procedures that would screen out apparently groundless claims, as well as restraints on the size of the contingent fee that an attorney could charge the patient to undertake claims with riskier prospects for recovery.
- Once a malpractice suit has entered the legal system, the common-law principles for appraising the merits of the injured patient's claim—in particular, the law's reliance on the customary standards of practice developed within the medical profession to define the legal standard of care—are considerably more favorable to doctors than they are to other tort defendants (including, for example, a manufacturer of prescription drugs who may be the target of a product liability suit brought by a patient in tandem with a malpractice claim against the doctor who prescribed the drug). With the exception, then, of some modest attempts to tie down specific features of such doctrines as informed consent, *res ipsa loquitur* ("the case speaks for itself"), and the locality standard, legislatures have not materially altered the common-law ground rules developed by the courts.

• Much broader statutory revisions have been made in the common-law principles for calculating the damages payable to injured patients by doctors who do violate the medico-legal standard of care. In this regard, medical liability has served as the proving ground for damage restraints that a number of state legislatures have since required for tort litigation generally. The most important such measures are: (1) offsetting against the malpractice award any payments received by the injured victim from collateral sources of loss insurance (such as insurance for medical expenses or lost earnings); (2) mandating that large awards for projected future losses be paid periodically as the losses occur, so that the award will terminate if the injured victim dies earlier than anticipated (note that only two states have made this innovation reciprocal, by requiring the periodic payment to continue if a particular victim happens to live longer than the actuarial expectancy at time of trial); and (3) a fixed dollar cap on the size of the tort award, whether the cap limits the amount of the entire award (as it does in a few states, such as Indiana) or only the amount payable for "pain and suffering" and other forms of nonpecuniary harm (as in California).

The state of New York rejected such fixed dollar caps as unfair to the most seriously injured victims, whose claims are the only ones constrained by a monetary ceiling (which is, moreover, rarely adjusted to later inflation). However, the state responded to the legitimate defendant concern about the "maverick" jury award by authorizing judges to review and revise any award that appeared to "deviate materially from what would be reasonable compensation for the case." This new statutory standard has generated much more active judicial scrutiny and revision of jury awards (revision occasionally upward as well as downward) than has the traditional judicial criterion of whether the jury's award "shocked the conscience of the court."

QUALITY ASSURANCE IN HEALTH CARE
State legislatures naturally have also been concerned about reducing the incidence of doctor carelessness and patient injuries in the first place, rather than merely constraining the frequency of tort claims

and the amount of tort awards that eventually flow from negligent treatment. New York has been one of the pacesetters in adopting measures to help foster better quality assurance within health care.

- Hospitals in various states have been required to institute thorough evaluation of physician competence before granting staff privileges to new doctors; periodically to review and upgrade the credentials and competence of their staff; to identify, investigate, and report all adverse incidents in patient treatment; and to hear and resolve patient grievances concerning the quality of care.
- Health care organizations (both physicians' associations and medical centers) have been prodded to develop and promulgate clinical practice guidelines and protocols to be followed in recurring risky procedures.
- State health departments have expanded and invigorated their offices of professional medical conduct, whose responsibility it is to monitor information about physician performance derived from malpractice insurers, hospital incident-reporting systems, and patient complaints, and to suspend or revoke a doctor's license (or at least restrict the scope of clinical practice) in any case in which there is a pattern of poor-quality care.

The Challenge for Empirical Research

Once these ambitious legislative programs were in force, serious empirical studies were done on the effects of the statutory reforms. In particular, noted scholars such as Patricia Danzon and Frank Sloan sought to document the impact of the tort measures enacted in the mid-1970s on malpractice claims and payments made in the mid-1980s.[10]

The verdict from this research was reasonably clear. Only a modest benefit could be observed as the result of legislation that aimed to modify either patient access to the tort system or the way that the tort system determined provider liability. Almost all the visible impact stemmed from measures that reduced or capped the size of the damage award. In fact, measures of this type not only directly reduced the average payments for settled claims but also indirectly reduced the frequency of initial claims by cutting back on the expected return from cases that appeared more difficult to sustain. Of course, even the most restrictive forms of state legislation enacted in the 1970s served only to contain the relative rate of increase in malpractice claims and premiums into the 1980s, rather than to reduce these premium rates absolutely. But the scientific message is that if the legislature wants to constrain malpractice costs, the most effective way to do so is to cap damage awards.[11] Unhappily, the damage cap also strikes many people as the most inequitable legislative solution, because the entire burden of malpractice cost containment is imposed on those patients who suffer the severest injuries and thus have the greatest needs.

The deeper problem with all these legislative enactments and research findings is that they tacitly and unquestioningly assume that malpractice litigation is an evil, such that even if political factors prevented total repeal of the system, tort liability should be whittled down as much as possible. That judgment may ultimately be valid. It is evident that the litigation process exacts substantial direct financial costs—an estimated $7 billion a year in premiums and self-insurance—and that it imposes considerable economic and psychological burdens on providers and payors in the health care system. But what has been sorely lacking in legislative debate about malpractice reform has been vital information about whether and to what extent malpractice litigation generates for patients treated within our vast medical complex a benefit that outweighs that heavy burden.

How many people are injured as a result of medical intervention, and how many of these injuries could have been avoided? What kinds of losses did patients suffer as a result of these medical injuries, and how much of the total loss was left uncovered by other forms of insurance? What influence does the prospect of medical malpractice litigation have in reducing the incidence and severity of injuries to future patients? Only when we have reliable answers to these questions can we make sensible judgments about whether the direct and indirect costs exacted by malpractice litigation are a worthwhile investment in improving the quality of performance within our $800-billion-a-year health care system, or whether better techniques exist for pursuing that goal.

Precisely in order to fill this information gap in the debate about medical liability, in 1986 the New York State legislature mandated a systematic empirical investigation of the extent of medical injury, the extent to which such injuries are compensated, and the feasibility of medical compensation systems that compensate victims irrespective of fault. This book is our response to that mandate. We hope that the much calmer malpractice atmosphere of today will permit more considered reflection on the significance of our findings.

CHAPTER 2

The Policy Debate about Medical Malpractice

The principal aim of the Harvard Medical Practice Study was to conduct a systematic empirical investigation of what New York's medical and legal systems are actually doing with respect to medical injuries, rather than to engage in normative evaluation of what they should be doing. For the last two decades New York State and the country as a whole have been well supplied with heated moralizing about medical malpractice, often conducted from starkly opposed perspectives and usually based on anecdotal evidence. Indeed, when our own team of doctors, economists, statisticians, and lawyers was assembled for this project, a considerable range of views existed among us about the best way to respond to the human problems of medical injury and legal response. Our comparative advantage obviously consisted in doing serious research and analysis of the crucial factual assumptions underlying the policy debate.

At the same time, we recognized that empirical research in any area of public policy cannot be conducted in a vacuum: it must be connected to the policy controversies that need factual illumination. So as a prelude to our inquiry we had to immerse ourselves in the current debate about medical malpractice law and seek to understand the sharply contrasting views that are regularly expressed about the tort system and possible alternatives. We found profound divisions on these issues not only in the political arena but also in the scholarly literature, and not only with respect to medical accidents but also respecting the broader field of personal injuries from consumer products, motor vehicles, the workplace, and other sources. To make clear why we made the crucial research decisions that we did, it is useful at this point to state as succinctly and as fairly as we can the nature of that debate.[1]

The Tort System

Medical practice and injuries are governed by certain well-established principles of the common-law tort system that also define liability for motor vehicle and consumer product (but not workplace) injuries.

- If a patient is injured as a result of the wrongful behavior of another (a physician or other medical care provider),[2] then the victim is entitled to recover for all losses—both financial and nonpecuniary—caused by such fault.
- In the absence of negligent behavior, a doctor is not legally responsible for injuries suffered by his or her patients; instead, such losses must be borne by the victims personally or by the broader community through its various programs of public and private loss insurance.
- Disputes over whether an instance of medical treatment was careless and over what injuries the victim suffered as a result are ultimately resolvable in a civil trial before a jury, although in practice some 90 percent of such claims are settled by the parties and their lawyers through voluntary negotiation before a trial.
- If some legal fault and liability are established through this process, compensation will almost invariably be paid to the victim not by the individual who was careless, but rather by a liability insurer for an independently practicing doctor or by the institution that employed the doctor or other provider in question (or by that institution's insurer).

This system of fault-based tort liability has traditionally been credited with securing two distinct though generally compatible objectives. First, the values of corrective justice and fairness require that losses that have already occurred as a result of careless action should be shifted (as far as is possible) from the innocent patient-victim to the culpable party.[3] Second, the prospect of being sued and having to pay for such losses will serve as a financial and emotional incentive to doctors to provide more careful treatment to their patients in the future.[4] The flip side of this policy rationale for the fault system is that if a patient injury was produced as a purely accidental by-product of careful medical treatment, imposing liability is not justified. To do so would unfairly single out innocent doctors (from among everyone else in the community) to bear financial responsibility for the plight of their injured patients, and could not deter substandard care because poor care was not the reason for imposing liability.

The foregoing is, we believe, a fair statement of the core assumptions of the common law of tort–fault liability. Among legal scholars, however, the corrective justice rationale is no longer in general favor. A principal reason is that with the emergence of widespread, often mandatory liability insurance, the careless doctor no longer pays the tort bill for the patient's injuries. Instead, the individual doctor's insurer pays the tort award with funds accumulated from liability insurance premiums paid by all doctors in the relevant specialty and region. In fact, in New York the excess insurance (coverage for liability in excess of $1 million per case) for physician malpractice is now provided and paid by the hospital with which the doctor is associated. In turn, doctors (and hospitals) pay for their often sizable insurance premiums with money collected from patients for medical services. And the vast majority of these doctors' fees are actually paid by private or public health insurance programs funded by premiums charged to individuals and employers or by taxes collected by governments. In other words, we now have an elaborate set of insurance arrangements in which healthy citizens are required, in effect, to purchase a form of disability insurance against the risk of at least some injuries arising out of their medical treatment.

Tort litigation, then, serves as a port of entry into this socially generated disability fund by determining which injured patients are to collect and how much. From that perspective, traditional concerns about securing corrective justice as between an injured victim and an individually culpable actor have little relevance. Rather, a more pragmatic policy analysis would be appropriate, one that would address the following questions:

How sensibly does the entire tort system distribute compensation to injured patients from the funds contributed by the broader constituency of the health care system?

How economic is administration of this disability insurance program in terms of money, time, and emotional demands on the parties?

How effective is such a program in preventing substandard medical treatment, so that all patients may be protected from iatrogenic injuries before they occur?

COMPENSATION

The tort system is designed to compensate all losses of patient-victims injured through the fault of their doctors, but in fact it compensates no losses of injured patients who cannot establish physician culpability. Tort critics charge that this substantive policy accounts for two crucial deficiencies of the system as a vehicle for compensatory insurance.[5]

The most obvious flaw concerns the plight of patients who recover nothing after suffering severe injuries, even though the injuries create real needs for financial help to pay for additional medical care and rehabilitation and to serve as a source of income during the period when the patient is unable to work. The needs of the injured patient are exactly the same irrespective of whether the carelessness of a doctor contributed to the original incident. Thus, from this perspective it seems arbitrary and unfair to deny this large category of needy victims any access at all to the disability insurance fund that has been accumulated in the manner described.

More recently, tort law has been charged with a second, contrasting defect. The commitment to full compensation of victims who establish the fault prerequisite appears to some to be incompatible with sound principles of loss insurance.[6] The most apparent violation of these principles occurs when large, unconstrained monetary damages are awarded for such essentially nonpecuniary losses as pain and suffering or loss of companionship. A similar failing appears in the right to full replacement of all lost earnings or treatment costs without any application of the deductible or coinsurance formulas that are standard in both private and public insurance.[7] Although there are historic reasons for this dichotomy in the tort regime between full compensation and no compensation, such a substantive policy simply cannot be justified as a sensible insurance program.

ADMINISTRATION

Irrespective of whether any substantive grounds can be advanced for the fault principle, it is clear that the fault ingredient entails a substantial administrative burden for the tort system. To make the crucial judgment about whether the doctor was careless involves reconstruction of an event that occurred years earlier, and a contest between expert witnesses trying to educate a lay jury about how to assess what are often complex and subtle questions about the appropriate standard of medical care. Even if such judgments can be made accurately and reliably (an assumption that much of the medical community vigorously rejects,[8] and about which we will provide some evidence later), the litigation process is certainly expensive in terms of time and money. Malpractice insurers in New York now spend an average of well over $10,000 to defend every malpractice claim, meritorious or not, while successful patient-claimants pay their own lawyers a fee that is generally one-third or more of the total award. Thus, even when one leaves aside the cost of securing and investing insurance funds and focuses simply on the process of claims administration and distribution, only about 40 percent of the total amount expended in the claims process actually reaches injured patients as compensation for their injuries.[9]

PREVENTION

Even defenders of the tort system would generally concede that this program is not a particularly sensible or economic mode of insurance and compensation. In their view, however, the admitted problems created by hinging the patient's compensation on proof of the doctor's negligence are a price worth paying in the effort to deter careless medical practice by all doctors. The response from critics of the tort system is that malpractice litigation is actually not an effective instrument for improving the quality of medical care.

There are two aspects to this critique. One is that any monetary sanction that is imposed upon a negligent doctor itself depends on the fortuitous occurrence and severity of the patient's injuries, rather than on the degree of the doctor's culpability. For example, a momentary inadvertent slip by a surgeon who is ordinarily attentive and meticulous, but whose mistake in this case inflicts permanent long-term brain damage on a patient, can make this doctor liable for millions of dollars in tort damages.[10] On the other hand, another doctor whose deviation from appropriate standards of care is both deliberate and egregious, but whose patient suffers a much less serious injury (or no injury), will escape with only moderate financial liability (or none at all). Indeed, unless the potential recoverable damages are reasonably large, there will be no liability in practice, because neither the patient nor a lawyer will have sufficient incentive to make the substantial initial investment required to institute a suit against the doctor.

In fact, the tort litigation system does not operate in accordance with the formal legal principle that would produce such discordant results. A liability insurer actually pays all these awards, whether large or small. What doctors pay is a standardized insurance premium that depends on the nature of their specialty and geographic location. But the presence of liability insurance in the background has attracted even sharper criticism of the deterrent rationale for the tort system. If careless doctors do not personally bear the cost of their negligence, then how can the prospect of a tort award effectively serve as a deterrent against substandard care by others? One might, of course, adjust the size of the doctor's insurance premium in light of individual claims experience (as New York State is now attempting to do).[11] However, there is considerable doubt whether a meaningful and actuarially credible experience rating program can be devised for liability insurance against malpractice claims, which occur so rarely for an individual doctor (by contrast, for example, with the much more extensive workers' compensation experience of a large employer).[12]

Still, to suggest that liability insurance fully insulates doctors from the impact of the tort system is somewhat unrealistic. A far more significant factor than even a demerit adjustment in an insurance premium is the loss of practice time and earnings, as well as personal morale and professional reputation, when the quality of the doctor's medical care is attacked through tort litigation.[13] The problem is that many of these costs are visited upon doctors from the mere act of being sued, not only in cases in which they are found liable. So in fact the tort system inflicts its tangible, uninsured sanctions on the majority of doctors whose degree of care is eventually vindicated, but whose patients have sought to use this legal avenue to secure financial redress for their serious injuries. A final critique of the tort system, then, is that its deterrent instrument is much too crude in operation: that it serves primarily to induce unnecessary and wasteful modes of defensive medicine designed to decrease doctors' likelihood of being sued rather than patients' likelihood of being cured.[14]

Alternatives to Tort

Finding fault with the tort system's inability to meet certain lofty but abstract ideals is rather easy. A much tougher challenge is to devise a system that could do a better job of securing our various, often incompatible goals.

To consider fundamental alternatives to *tort-fault liability* (rather than just the specific reforms that New York has made in its tort system, as described in Chapter 1), one might move in either of two directions. In one direction lies the *no-liability* option, under which the tort system would be dismantled (perhaps through private contract)[15] and injured patients would pursue redress through the same public and private systems of loss insurance that are available to victims of any other disabling injury. Proponents of this type of policy often advocate considerably improved systems of social insurance for medical costs and lost earnings, and stiffer regulatory sanctions against risky behavior.[16] Of course, one implication of this no-liability option is that providers of medical care would shoulder no special burden to pay for the losses suffered by the patient-victims of accidents occasioned by medical care.

The opposite path would take us from fault to *no-fault* (or *strict*) *liability*. Under a regime of no-fault medical accident insurance (provided on a mandatory or a voluntary basis by private or by public carriers), legal responsibility for adverse consequences of medical treatment would still be discharged through a special program devised and paid for within the health care system. A patient's entitlement to compensation would turn not on whether the doctor had been at fault, however, but simply on the fact that the injury had been caused by medical treatment. By analogy to no-fault workers' compensation, the crucial test in such a patient compensation program would not be whether someone could be blamed for the injury, but simply whether the injury "arose out of and in the course of" medical treatment.

The no-fault option surfaced in the debate about medical malpractice in the early 1970s as a consequence of dissatisfaction with the performance of the tort system.[17] New Zealand adopted a version of categorical no-fault compensation for the victims of medical accidents as a feature of its broader social insurance approach to all accidental injuries.[18] Sweden followed with a separate and self-contained patient compensation scheme.[19] In 1975 the members of New York's McGill Advisory Panel on Medical Malpractice endorsed the idea in principle.

However, because a number of significant difficulties impeded the creation and implementation of no-fault patient compensation, this option stayed largely in the background while the debate focused on a variety of tort reforms. With the resurgence of malpractice litigation and premium costs in the 1980s, not just in the United States but elsewhere in the world as well,[20] the no-fault idea came back into vogue. Finland adopted a program largely modeled on Sweden's,[21] the British Medical Association has expressed interest in this idea,[22] and a federal-provincial commission in Canada recently proposed adoption of no-fault there.[23] Meanwhile, in this country the states of Virginia and Florida have adopted no-fault compensation schemes for infants who suffer severe and permanent brain damage during obstetrical delivery, a class of injury that poses major problems for the present medical malpractice system.[24] In this setting, New York commissioned our study of the respective values of the no-fault and tort-fault approaches to medical accidents.

The literature on the no-fault alternative makes it clear that although this model has significant comparative advantages over tort–fault, it also has considerable problems of its own. On the positive side, the virtues of no-fault are particularly responsive to the deficiencies we saw in the tort system.[25]

COMPENSATION

The scope of this disability insurance would be broadened to cover the victims of all medical injuries, not just injured patients "lucky" enough to be able to prove that their injuries resulted from the negligence of a doctor or some other financially responsible provider.

At the same time, at least if the coverage were based on the philosophy (though not necessarily the specifics) of the no-fault model in the workplace, the amount of compensation paid to any one victim would probably be scaled downward—particularly with respect to pain and suffering, but also with respect to some proportion of lost earnings. This reduction would be justified in part because it would free up some of the funds needed to finance the expanded coverage for all victims, and in part because (for reasons alluded to earlier) such a compensation format is more in accord with sound insurance principles.

ADMINISTRATION
Elimination of the legal contest over the crucial tort issue of whether a doctor was at fault would remove one major source of litigation. Disputes would still arise over the patient's entitlement to any compensation and over the size of the award, but these disputes would focus on the more technical questions of the precise source and extent of the patient's injury rather than on whether the doctor was to blame for what happened. This change would spare both doctor and patient the emotional and financial costs of a heated legal conflict and permit the community to shift a large portion of resources now spent on lawyers, expert witnesses, and court personnel to direct reimbursement of injured patients for the losses they suffer.

PREVENTION
These compensatory and administrative values could obviously be served even better by dispensing entirely with the requirement of "cause" as a predicate for patient recovery and adopting instead a broader social insurance approach to meeting the patient's needs.[26] It might seem illogical to establish a program guaranteeing patients insurance compensation for the health care costs from disabling injuries incurred inside the hospital, when there is no such guarantee of health insurance coverage for the injuries or illnesses that brought the patients into the hospital in the first place. However, there is an important rationale for adopting a specific no-fault program for a separate category of injuries caused by an activity such as health care, even though such a categorical program would entail significant compromises in the easy and evenhanded compensation of past

injuries. A no-fault program would keep within the medical care system itself the legal responsibility for injuries that result from its operations; this legal burden would serve as a significant financial incentive inside the system to provide safer care and more effective prevention of future injuries to all patients.

This is the crucial difference between the model of no liability even where there is fault (referred to earlier) and the model of strict liability irrespective of fault considered here. Under a no-fault regime, the doctor (more likely the hospital) is subject to essentially the same legal and financial responsibility that tort law imposes for injuries that could and should have been avoided by more careful treatment—the fault-caused injuries. Consequently, to the extent that the prospect of such liability furnishes any meaningful incentive to providers to take greater care, the existing legal incentives would be largely untouched if such awards were paid under a no-fault scheme. No-fault imposes even broader liability on the medical care system by requiring that it pay for patient losses from iatrogenic injuries that do not currently appear to be avoidable by feasible methods. This additional legal responsibility would embed within the health care system a powerful incentive to develop innovative quality assurance techniques and equipment that would make it feasible to avoid more and more of the medical accident toll.

Given the apparent advantages of no-fault, it is reasonable to ask why this model has not been taken seriously in the medical arena as the burdens of the tort liability regime have seemingly become more and more oppressive. One answer is that even those who are generally sympathetic to no-fault—in the domain of motor vehicle accidents, for example—have several reservations about the merits of such a program for medical injuries.[27]

COST
An obvious concern is the potential financial burden of having to compensate all patient injuries under a no-fault scheme. Modern medical care is an inherently risky enterprise. The major precursor to our own empirical study, the *Medical Insurance Feasibility Study* in California in the mid-1970s,[28] found the risk of disabling injury to patients to be roughly 1 in 20 hospital admissions. Only a small

fraction of these injuries produced actual tort recoveries under the fault principle. Yet all such iatrogenic injuries would theoretically be eligible for compensation under a no-fault scheme. Thus, because the primary motivation for reform efforts in the malpractice arena has been to stem spiraling liability insurance premiums, adoption of a no-fault program, which would add a host of new claims for compensation, has seemed to be precisely the opposite direction to take.

CAUSE

Although substituting cause for fault as the precondition to compensation does broaden the potential range of patient recovery, a no-fault scheme would nonetheless retain an intrinsic limit on which injuries would be the financial responsibility of such a patient compensation program. Administration of the new compensability borderline is a second area of serious concern.

We noted earlier that under no-fault workers' compensation the standard inquiry is whether the worker's injury "arose out of and in the course of employment." In the case of workplace accidents use of this formula has occasioned little practical difficulty.[29] Unfortunately, no such simple formula will work in the medical area.

By comparison with workplace accidents, in which the employee typically goes to work healthy and leaves hurt, the patient who goes to a doctor or hospital is already in an unhealthy condition, often requiring medical intervention that can itself be traumatic in character. Severe difficulties can then arise in distinguishing disabling injuries that actually were the adverse consequence of medical care (such as an infection resulting from conditions in the operating room) from those that were attributable to the original illness (an infection caused by the original wound). And even if the disability is clearly attributable to the treatment, the patient would not necessarily have a right to compensation, because some such traumatic effects may be the inevitable by-product of treatment that was in the patient's broader interests: consider, for instance, the removal of a cancerous limb or organ. In light of examples such as these, most commentators have been dubious that the precise (and compensable) medical contribution could be reliably disentangled from the many other factors that may produce a patient's ultimate disability. They doubt at least that this distinction can be made with greater ease and economy than it is now under the tort system, using fault as the predicate for recovery. Moreover, in a no-fault system the number of claims for which such a determination would have to be made would be considerably greater. As a result, the anticipated savings in administration and litigation expenses under a no-fault program might be far from great enough to cover the broader scope of compensation.

CARE

A final concern is that the adoption of no-fault in the medical arena would unduly dilute the necessary incentives for safe treatment. As we saw earlier, a no-fault scheme would place on the health care system the legal responsibility for medical injuries, thus providing a significant financial incentive to prevent injuries that can be avoided by reasonable efforts.[30] However, there are a number of important differences in the way that the tort and the no-fault liability systems function with respect to encouraging high standards of care.

- Although the overall financial cost of no-fault might well be higher because the system would compensate all injured patients regardless of fault, the amount paid to those who *are* the victims of careless treatment would undoubtedly be lower than under the full-compensation principle of the tort regime. Consequently, the financial incentive to avoid *negligent* incidents (to the extent that they could even be isolated within the broader universe of cases facing the provider) would be significantly reduced.
- Again, if the workplace example were followed, no-fault medical accident insurance would more likely be provided and paid for by organizations such as hospitals, clinics, and health management organizations (HMOs) rather than by the individual doctors who provide the treatment and whose personal carelessness may be the actual cause of a patient's injury.
- Irrespective of who pays for the patient's losses (as the liability insurer does under the current tort system), a more important difference under no-fault is that the outside public would no longer have the opportunity, through the jury trial, to scrutinize the behavior of doctors and hospital staff, and perhaps to condemn

practices that are inappropriate. To the extent, then, that the beneficial influence of the fault-based tort system is traceable more to subtle factors of moral pressures than to direct pecuniary expenditures, much of that influence would be lost under no-fault.

• Another common concern about no-fault is that it obscures the responsibility and culpability of the individual victim in the occurrence of many accidents. Although the patient in the hospital typically plays a more passive role in medical accidents than does the employee in the workplace or the consumer-user in a product-related case, a considerable number of medical injuries—including many arising from the use of prescription drugs—could be avoided by greater patient care and attention to the doctor's instructions. One fear about no-fault is that a guarantee of compensation will reduce the patient's instinct for self-preservation (including, *inter alia,* the risks of aggressive medical treatment), and as a result add to the injury toll within the hospital and the cost burden on the patient compensation scheme.

• Finally, many critics lament the tendency of the tort system to encourage wasteful defensive measures on the part of the individual physician seeking to erect a barrier to litigation; and hospitals might respond in a similar way if they were made financially responsible for a no-fault compensation scheme for the benefit of their patients. As we shall see in Chapter 3, patients are by no means homogeneous with respect to their risk of suffering iatrogenic injury. Some hospitals may be tempted to reduce their financial exposure to such insurance costs by refusing to admit those categories of patients who are most likely to experience adverse events. That reaction would be similar to the patient dumping that is said to take place within the incentive structure of Medicare's new Prospective Payment System.[31]

The general theme pervading these several concerns is that medical no-fault would inevitably function in too unobtrusive and impersonal a fashion, focusing only on the financial responsibility of the enterprise. Such a system would fall far short of the morality play of tort litigation, with its emphasis on the personal blame and accountability of human beings, in galvanizing the health care system into making serious efforts to eliminate substandard care.

The Research Agenda

The foregoing is merely a brief sketch of the arguments that are made for and against two contrasting liability systems for dealing with medical injuries. Experts on the subject will appreciate the necessary qualifications and available responses to the opposing claims we have set out; they will also realize that any real-life program, fault-based or no-fault, can be refined to accommodate at least some of these concerns. Our objective at this point is not to take a stand in favor of one position or another in this policy debate, but rather to underscore that real issues and arguments exist on both sides. Further, lurking beneath the surface of the polarized positions are some crucial factual assumptions—about the incidence of medical injuries and carelessness, about the needs of injured patients for compensation, and about the legal incentives for greater care in medical treatment. These assumptions often have little or no factual basis and, as we shall see, may be misguided. The aim of our research has been to investigate each of the key empirical dimensions of the policy problem.

The details of our research efforts are described in succeeding chapters. Here it will be useful to state them in broad outline. We studied the hospital records of a statewide sample of roughly 30,000 patients in New York hospitals in 1984. Through a careful review of these records, we determined which admissions produced adverse consequences from the medical services rendered, which of such consequences were due to the fault of a doctor or other provider, and, in those cases, the degree of such fault (ranging from minimal to severe).

After determining which hospital admissions involved iatrogenic injuries, we conducted a survey of the affected patients to ascertain the financial and personal consequences of the injuries (as compared to a control group of patients who were not injured). What kinds of additional medical costs were incurred? What extra losses of earnings were experienced? What impairments were suffered in the ability to function in the household and in regular nonwork activities? How many of these losses were actually compensated through the variety of existing programs, private as well as public, tort as well as nontort?

A third area of inquiry was to assess the response of the tort system to these events, with respect to both the doctor and the patient. What was the level and distribution of tort claims arising from our entire sample of cases, including those we judged not to be negligent adverse events? What consequences, financial and psychological, do tort proceedings tend to have on a doctor personally (as opposed to the effects on the doctor's insurer), and what are the apparent consequences to the doctor's subsequent practice? And finally, could econometric analysis tell us whether the considerable variation in the risk faced by New York doctors in the different regions of the state had any discernible preventive impact on the rate of injury in our overall sample of 30,000 admissions in that year?

Each component of the overall research project has produced data important for a variety of perspectives on the medical injury problem. For example, our systematic review of a large sample of hospital admissions enabled us to develop a comprehensive epidemiological picture of iatrogenic injuries: the kinds of patients and disease conditions; the types of doctors, other providers, and hospitals; and the variety of medical procedures and settings that are especially accident prone. Such material is crucial for those responsible for quality assurance within the medical system, giving them clues to the underlying causes of such accident patterns and suggesting where they should place their priorities. It does little good for tort litigation or other external legal regimes to escalate the legal sanctions against substandard care if those who are actually practicing within the health care system cannot obtain the information necessary to devise the practice protocols and safeguards that could produce a significant reduction in adverse outcomes.

But over and above the contribution this study could make to directly enhancing the quality of care within the medical system, our research was designed to shed light on the key issues disputed by the proponents of fault and no-fault liability.

AFFORDABILITY

We noted earlier that the first question that arises in considering whether no-fault coverage is viable for medical accidents is whether it would be financially affordable. Yet from a more fundamental perspective, this is a spurious question. Once a medical injury has occurred and losses are suffered by a patient, the losses must be borne and thus "afforded" somehow, either by the patient personally or by some other segment of the community. Still, any consideration of whether to alter the nature of the health care system's own responsibility for such injuries requires information about the cost of the insurance that would be needed. And particularly because the *Medical Insurance Feasibility Study* in California found that only a small fraction of the substantial number of victims of iatrogenic injuries recovered anything in tort actions, the obvious objection to no-fault patient compensation is that it would generate far too steep an increase in already burdensome malpractice insurance premiums.

However, the potential costs of a no-fault program cannot be estimated simply from data on how many patients were injured and what proportion of these cases arose through negligence or purely through accident. It is also necessary to know the size of the losses those injuries caused patients, particularly those losses that a no-fault program would be likely to compensate. The extent of a disabled patient's earnings loss, for example, depends not only on the occurrence but also on the severity of the physical impairment and, even more, on the interaction of this impairment with the age, occupation, and other personal characteristics of the victim.[32] It is possible that a large share of the more costly accidents is actually caused by negligent treatment—cases that are potentially litigable under the tort system. If that were true, it would decrease the gap between total patient losses and those that would be potentially compensable under no-fault. The major aim of the patient survey, then, was to learn from the patients themselves what losses they had suffered and how such losses were distributed between fault and no-fault accidents.

This is still just one side of the equation: it is also necessary to know how much of these losses the program needs to compensate. Let us assume that no-fault patient insurance would be a secondary source of compensation, serving as a backstop to the general medical disability insurance provided by a range of private and public programs (a role that medical malpractice insurance itself now plays in New York, following the reversal of the collateral source rule). In that case estimates of the cost of such insurance require knowledge not just of the losses the patients have suffered, but also of what alternative sources of insurance coverage they had and how much of their losses was made up from those sources.

Furthermore, one must not assume that all these net losses must be compensated in full. From a purely insurance perspective it would make sense to exclude the numerous shorter-term disabling injuries on the assumption that these relatively modest losses can and should be covered by the victim's personal resources. Priority in any insurance program should always be given to the longer-lasting disabilities that affect far fewer patients but inflict severe or even catastrophic losses on the individual and family concerned.[33] In other words, it is possible to design a no-fault program that would target benefits and expenditures toward the needier cases, which should have first claim on the available resources. But in order to make realistic estimates of the potential costs of different versions of a patient insurance program, it is necessary to have detailed information from a survey of patients on the distribution as well as the aggregate size of the net losses suffered from disabling medical injuries.

ADMINISTRABILITY

A second concern arises with respect to the tort system as well as a possible no-fault substitute: each such regime requires a difficult judgment about their respective legal conditions for patient entitlement to compensation. The tort system consumes large quantities of emotion as well as money in the adversarial contest over whether a doctor was at fault as a predicate to awarding an injured patient any redress.[34] By contrast, the no-fault model in workers' compensation expends roughly 20 percent of its claims dollar on administration, or roughly one-third the proportion spent in medical malpractice.[35] It is likely, however, that any attempt to transplant the no-fault model into the medical area would encounter a greater administrative burden in its inquiry over cause, since there is an inherent difficulty in disentangling adverse consequences that are the accidental by-products of medical treatment from the disabling effects of the initial illness or of appropriate treatment procedures.

In fact, those who have reported on the experience with patient compensation plans in Sweden and New Zealand find that this problem is not as great in practice as it threatens to be in principle. In those countries a number of conceptual and pragmatic difficulties have been encountered; these have gradually been resolved through a detailed jurisprudence. However, the reports we have read indicate that these systems have operated reasonably well, with doctors able to help their injured patients to collect the benefits to which they are entitled rather than obliged to defend their professional reputation against allegations of negligence.[36]

However, the only way we could be confident about this issue in the New York context was actually to look at the cases there. So in our systematic survey of adverse events and negligence we instructed our reviewers not simply to give us a bottom-line judgment about whether there was "cause" or "fault" displayed in the medical records, but also to record the degree of difficulty that they encountered in making those judgments. We were then able to make firmer estimates not just of the existence of the cause-determination problem, but also of its dimensions—how many close calls had to be made about the causation of adverse events? Moreover, we were able to assess the extent of the problem not just in absolute terms, but also by comparison with the degree of difficulty in judging the negligence of the doctor. Finally, the very large number of the cases in our sample enabled us to determine whether the threshold cases tended to occur at random or in recurring patterns that would enable a policymaker to specify certain formulas for designating an event as adverse and compensable or not.

CONTROLLABILITY

Whatever may be the verdict about the affordability and the administrability of a particular program for compensating past medical injuries, an equally important policy concern is to what extent the program would reduce the future incidence of medical injuries. We cannot produce empirical evidence for that role in the case of no-fault patient compensation, because no such plan now exists in New York (although we noted earlier the substantial effect that no-fault workers' compensation has in reducing workplace injuries).[37] On the other hand, we did attempt to gather systematic evidence about the preventive effect of existing tort litigation on medical accidents in the state, because prevention has to be the major justification of the tort regime.

Four aspects of our research program were pertinent to the prevention issue. The review of medical records disclosed whether the primary source of iatrogenic injuries (and of the more seriously disabling injuries in particular) was provider negligence or whether the injuries were purely accidental by-products of medical treatment. In addition, the reviewers tried to make more specific judgments about the degree of carelessness displayed in these cases and to what extent the careless behavior might be influenced by the legal context. Next, our analysis of tort claims compared the reactions of the tort process with the judgments we had made about provider negligence and adverse events in our sample. How often were tort suits brought by our patients, and were they brought in the appropriate cases? How well did the distribution of such claims correlate with the seriousness of the doctor's negligence rather than with the severity of the patient's disability and needs? Then our physician survey sought to cast light on how doctors react to the experience or the threat of being sued: do the signal and the sanction emitted by the legal system elicit changes in the way individuals practice medicine?

We then attempted to see whether any deterrent impact of the tort system on physician behavior was manifested in turn in the incidence and distribution of patient injuries, rather than in reported physician perceptions. Our data base of a state-wide sample of adverse and negligent adverse events made it possible to conduct the first econometric investigation of whether medical malpractice litigation actually reduces patient injuries. Because all the cases in our sample were formally subject to the identical tort law prevailing in New York at the time, we could not test directly the deterrent influence of that law by comparing the performance of a group subject to New York liability with the record of a control group that was not subject to the New York system. On the other hand, the observed *intensity* of tort litigation—the statistical likelihood that a suit would be filed against a doctor or hospital—was several times greater in some parts of the state than in others. Thus, as a proxy for the either/or, tort/no-tort possibility, we used the more-tort/less-tort variation across different hospitals and medical staffs to determine whether this variation produced any difference in measurable doctor negligence and patient injuries (controlling for other relevant characteristics of the patient, the illness, the hospital facilities, and so on) in the 30,000 cases from across the state. In Chapter 6 we discuss the serious statistical obstacles to teasing out any such relationship in the limited data base we had to work with.

Conclusion

The aim of our research program has been to inform the policy debate now going on in this country about how best to deal with medical accidents and malpractice. In order to make a meaningful contribution to this controversial subject, we had to understand and isolate the major issues and assumptions that divide the protagonists of the tort system and proponents of the no-fault alternatives to tort. Since there were pronounced differences of views about these issues among the members of the study team when we embarked on our research, as a group we had no affirmative position about the feasibility of a no-fault program for injured patients, nor did we endorse the criticisms that are made about the existing malpractice litigation system. Our principal aim was to generate the necessary empirical data that would permit better-informed judgments about the variety of charges and countercharges regularly exchanged by participants in the malpractice controversy. The next four chapters present our key findings. We reflect on their policy implications in the final chapter.

CHAPTER 3

The Epidemiology
of Medical Injury

Objectives

Securing accurate estimates of the incidence and patterns of medical injury or adverse events—or in health care parlance, iatrogenic injury—was the cornerstone of our research agenda, as it must be for intelligent policymaking in this area. The ultimate aims of both malpractice litigation and alternative policy instruments are to compensate victims and to reduce such injury. To approach those goals we needed to know the magnitude of the problem and in what medical settings it is most concentrated. Further, we wished to determine the efficacy of tort litigation in compensating patient losses and deterring inappropriate behavior on the part of providers. Finally, we regarded such information as vital to our additional, and perhaps most important, objective of helping to develop a comprehensive methodology for preventing medical injury.

The technique we employed for the studies of medical injury was an in-depth appraisal of the medical records of a carefully selected representative sample of 31,000 patients hospitalized in New York State in 1984. Through this record review we set out to identify which patients suffered iatrogenic injuries and which of these injuries were attributable to the negligence of a doctor or other health care provider.

Both our analyses and our research protocols were greatly assisted by the pioneering work of Dr. Don Harper Mills and his colleagues, who had completed a similar hospital record review in California more than a decade earlier. Their study was a landmark event, but it had certain methodological problems that we sought to remedy in

New York. In addition, our goal was to go far beyond an analysis of hospital records in order to generate the additional data needed for appraising the value of tort and its alternatives in compensating and preventing injuries.

To analyze the adverse event data themselves, we followed a systematic epidemiological approach to iatrogenic injury. At best, malpractice litigation or other legal alternatives can redress the financial consequences of injuries that have already occurred to patients and prod health care providers to adopt measures that will reduce the occurrence of such injuries. But it does little good for the law to impose sanctions, no matter how stiff and accurate, on doctors or hospital administrators who are not preventing injuries, if they do not know how to prevent them in the first place.

The starting point for knowing how to reduce medical injury is to know where these injuries occur and the factors most associated with them. The nascent quality assurance movement in American medicine has begun to make use of generic screening procedures to develop more systematic data about poor outcomes—for example, data about comparative hospital mortality rates. As we shall see later, the problem with such data is that they control crudely, if at all, for the sharply varying degrees of difficulty presented by different kinds of patients and conditions treated in, say, suburban hospitals as contrasted with university teaching hospitals. Such a methodological problem is largely ameliorated by in-depth analysis of a cross-section of hospital records to uncover both the incidence of iatrogenic injury and the percentage of such injury attributable to provider negligence. The second aim of our hospital record study, then, was to develop (for the first time) a body of such data for use in quality assurance programs, and in so doing to demonstrate the value of such ongoing self-examination and self-improvement for the inevitably risky processes of medical care.

Methods

CAUSATION AND NEGLIGENCE

The hospital record review sought to identify all adverse events suffered by patients in New York hospitals, as well as the subset of injuries attributable to the negligence of a doctor or other health care provider. There are ticklish practical and conceptual issues surrounding both causation and negligence in the context of medical treatment. Unlike people who get into a motor vehicle or go to work, most patients who go into a hospital are already sick, and the treatment they receive may itself be inherently traumatic. What we set out to discover were those adverse events that were the unintended or unexpected harmful consequences of medical intervention, and that prolonged the hospitalization beyond the time required by the underlying illness and/or caused disability at the time of hospital discharge or death. A negligent adverse event was the consequence of treatment that failed to meet the standard of the average medical practitioner in the field.[1] We also made judgments about the severity of a particular injury and the gravity of a doctor's negligence. In accordance with the approach in malpractice litigation itself, which relies heavily on medical custom and expert doctor testimony, we ultimately relied on the verdicts of physicians whom we had trained on each of these scores.

In the pilot phase of our work we gave a great deal of attention to the vexing questions of how to define and determine the relevant causes of a patient's injury and the presence of negligent treatment on the part of a provider. These issues have long been subject to debate in the jurisprudence of tort law, which under current malpractice doctrine grants redress only to patients who suffered an injury as a result of treatment that was careless in some fashion or other. For reasons explained in detail elsewhere,[2] many of these same problems would preoccupy administrators of a no-fault patient compensation plan. Thus, we had to address these issues ourselves as we sought to develop a comprehensive picture of the extent of medical injury that would be potentially compensable under such a plan.

As brief illustration of the problems, suppose that a patient's limb was amputated in the course of treatment for bone cancer. Although the immediate cause of this traumatic event would have been the medical intervention, the resulting disability would be properly attributable to the underlying illness, not to the actions of the health care provider who had deliberately taken this step to save the patient's life. What we looked for in the hospital record review, then, were the unintended and adverse consequences of medical management, not the inevitable consequences of proper intervention designed to remedy the underlying conditions. On the other hand, the risk that materialized did not have to be of a kind or likelihood that could have occurred only if the original treatment decision was negligent. Suppose, for example, that a coronary catheterization required by the patient's condition unfortunately precipitates a blood clot that travels to a patient's foot, where it cuts off the flow of blood, a rare event that also might require amputation. We would categorize this as a disability caused by the medical treatment, even though the course of treatment was proper, not negligent.

On the other hand, some adverse events that are physically caused by the illness itself—for example, death from breast cancer—would properly be attributable to the health care system if the system failed in its responsibility to diagnose accurately and select the appropriate treatment for the condition. Interestingly, then, in such cases of medical omission, the judgment about whether a patient's disability was caused by medical management actually rests on an implicit identification of fault on the part of some provider involved in care of the patient.

RELIABILITY AND VALIDITY
The same problems had been grappled with by Mills and his colleagues when they were carrying out their review of medical records in California.[3] After surveying some 20,000 hospital records of 1974 California patients, they found that adverse events—or potentially compensable events, as they were labeled—occurred in 4.65 percent (roughly 1 in 21) of hospitalizations, and negligent adverse events —or potentially litigable events—occurred in 0.79 percent (1 in 125) of hospitalizations (or 1 in 6 injuries).

The methodology developed by the California researchers served as an important model for us. They trained personnel to screen records for one of several defined outcomes. Records positive for such outcomes were then reviewed by a physician-lawyer who decided whether there was an adverse event and, if so, whether it was potentially litigable, and then estimated the disability caused by the injury. We relied heavily on the work of Mills and his colleagues, but we modified and extended their approach considerably. First, because their sample hospitals were volunteers rather than randomly selected, we were concerned that hospitals with concerns about having a higher incidence of negligence might be less likely to participate. That possibility introduced a risk of bias. Second, we addressed the issue of the reliability and reproducibility of the judgments made by the different people who screened and reviewed hospital records for us. Finally, the California study did not deal with the crucial question of the validity of the hospital record as an accurate portrayal of patient injuries or provider negligence. Outsiders are understandably skeptical about whether records kept by a hospital provide a true and systematic picture of the harmful outcomes of management within its walls.[4]

Before undertaking the major hospital record review, then, we carried out a number of pilot studies that addressed these questions. We trained medical record analysts (MRAs)—individuals with experience in compiling and analyzing hospital charts—to screen all records to see whether they contained evidence of one or more of 18 clinical criteria, such as previous hospitalization within one year, transfer to an intensive care unit, or death during hospitalization. The criteria we formulated are frequently associated with adverse outcomes but are simple enough to be readily documented from the chart itself by an MRA.[5] In a pilot study of this process, we concluded that only 1 in 200 adverse events was likely to be missed by this procedure.[6]

Records failing this MRA screen were then scrutinized in depth by at least two physicians who made independent judgments about medical injury, negligence, and level of disability caused by the injury. This phase also required careful attention to the issue of reliability, since earlier research by others had indicated that physician estimates (known technically as implicit physician judgments) of the causes of hospital mortality or morbidity could be quite subjective.[7] A substantial psychometric literature, however, indicates that greater reliability can be secured in such physician judgments through the use of a detailed standardized form.[8]

Consequently, we developed an Adverse Event Analysis Form (AEAF) that was designed to lead the reviewer through the hospital record review. A series of specific questions, developed with the help of medical experts we had interviewed, preceded all important judgments the reviewers had to make. We intended that each reviewer have in mind the same critical factors when deciding whether an adverse event or negligence had occurred. This permitted us to use surgeons and internists as reviewers, rather than the physician-lawyers who completed the review in California. (It also allows the study design to be widely used by health care institutions that could not or would not rely on physician-attorneys for quality assessment purposes.)

In a pilot study we estimated the extent of physician agreement about both causation and negligence. We found that doctors who were trained in the use of our elaborate Adverse Event Analysis Form made highly reliable judgments about causation—that is, about adverse events—while their judgments about carelessness—that is, about negligent adverse events—were reasonably reliable.[9] To improve performance we directed physicians to rank on a scale of 0 to 6 their own confidence in the judgments they had to make, ranging from virtual certainty in their verdict that there was causation or negligence to virtually complete confidence in their finding that there was none. Not only did this process give us an indication of the proportion of close calls in our sample—the usefulness of which we shall note later—but the fact that physicians were forced to think through their own judgments in this fashion promoted greater reliability in the overall process.

The most important concern, and the most elaborate pilot study, related to the value of the hospital record as a source of accurate and comprehensive information about adverse events and negligent care taking place within the hospital. To address that question we conducted an experiment in which we compared our reviewers' findings from patients' hospital records with independent verdicts about the same hospitalizations arrived at from much more comprehensive claims files for those patients whose hospitalizations had led to litigation. On the assumption that the tort claim's file could serve as a "gold standard," given that file's detailed investigation and personal interviews concerning the patient's treatment and injuries, we found that more than 80 percent of adverse events and nearly 75 percent of negligent adverse events were accurately identified from hospital records alone.[10] In addition, because physicians were just as likely to overidentify as to underidentify adverse events and negligence in the hospital records, we were satisfied that the records themselves gave a reasonably accurate picture of overall injury rates in the hospitals.

We recognized that reliance on hospital records would not permit us to evaluate all injuries occurring in the outpatient setting. While acknowledging this limitation in our study design, we are satisfied that the gap left by our inability to review ambulatory care is relatively small. First, many hospitals have integrated hospital/ambulatory records, which permitted us to review outpatient care for a considerable number of hospitalized patients. Further, because most significant disabling injuries inflicted by treatment outside the hospital—in a doctor's office, for example—will eventually lead to hospitalization, our hospital record review does provide a useful window on the risks of medical management outside. Finally, research by others on this issue suggests that the rate of iatrogenic injury in the ambulatory setting is small,[11] although the growing emphasis on early discharge and on ambulatory surgery may change this.

Another gap was created by patients whose injuries in one institution were not recognized until after discharge and who were then admitted to a different hospital. Such adverse events could not be traced to the first hospital unless it happened to have been one of the other fifty hospitals in our study. Though unlikely to introduce enormous bias in our results, this problem could affect our estimates of neonatal injury. For example, some infants injured as a result of lack of oxygen at birth may not demonstrate any symptoms for one to three years, when subtle neurological difficulties begin to appear. They may then be admitted to other institutions (if they are hospitalized at all) for diagnostic tests. Although our study design would miss these injuries, it did include an offsetting number of patients who had been injured in non-sample hospitals and then admitted to one of ours.

SAMPLE SELECTION

With an acceptable methodology for record review in hand, we then turned to sampling. We needed a sample of sufficient size to serve all aspects of the study: to allow us to make sturdy estimates of the number of medical injuries, to provide a sufficient number of injured individuals to interview about their subsequent losses, and to enable econometric estimates to be made of the deterrent effect of variations in the tort threat. The sample had to be large enough to permit statistically accurate estimates both of aggregate injury rates and of the injury distribution among different types of hospitals, different kinds of procedures, and different demographic groups. The rates of injury we observed in the California study, information concerning typical rates of participation in surveys, and the precision we desired led us to calculate a desired sample of roughly 31,000 records.

The number of medical records was only one sampling issue. To generalize the findings about 31,000 patients to the 2.6 million people hospitalized annually in New York State, we needed a random sample of patients. Further, while it was not practical to review records at every acute care, nonpsychiatric hospital in New York, we wanted a picture of the problem in rural and urban, teaching and nonteaching, government and nongovernment, nonprofit and for-profit institutions, and others. Therefore, we began by choosing a random sample of New York's hospitals. Moreover, we were able to obtain more precise estimates by oversampling high-risk patients and undersampling low-risk patients. In our analyses, of course, we re-weighted the findings to make them representative. Thus, some cases counted for more than one observation (those carrying a weight higher than 1) and others counted for less than one observation (those carrying a weight lower than 1). In addition, hospital units were carefully created using administrative data, and then enrolled consecutively into the sampling frame. With information provided by the state of New York,[12] this rather complicated sampling strategy identified 31,429 records in 51 hospitals.[13]

At the outset, we realized that if more than 3 or 4 of the 51 hospitals refused to take part, our overall results would be potentially biased. Fortunately, most hospitals quickly agreed to cooperate. Several others needed additional reassurance regarding the confidentiality of all information obtained in the medical record review. Eventually all 51 hospitals agreed to participate.

We chose 1984 as the year for which we would study the hospitalization experience and results. On the one hand, we wanted a year that was sufficiently recent that its conclusions about medical care and iatrogenic injury would still be relevant. On the other hand, sufficient time had to have elapsed after hospitalization that patients would have brought their malpractice claims and their losses from the medical injuries would have developed and stabilized.

The record review began in the summer of 1988. Teams of MRAs and physicians traveled to each hospital and reviewed the records of the selected hospitalizations. In most institutions it was possible to review other hospitalizations of the particular patient, and in some, outpatient records were also available. The initial review by MRAs using the 18 screening criteria eliminated about 70 percent of the records.

The remaining records were directed to physician-reviewers. Because of what we had learned from the reliability studies, we decided to perform two independent physician reviews of each record that screened positive. These reviewers filled out the Adverse Event Analysis Form for each record, spending an average of one-half hour on each case (in many instances spending over an hour on a single complicated case). Using the six-point confidence scale they decided whether there was "causation" (an injury caused by medical care as opposed to the disease process). Next, our reviewers gathered information from the record concerning location of injury, responsible clinical service, nature of the adverse event, and other issues. They then estimated the degree of physical disability, using a standard eight-point scale ranging from slight to fatal injury. Finally came the crucial decision of whether there had been substandard care by one or more providers.

Differences between the two reviewers on important issues were resolved by one of six senior physicians who were involved throughout this phase of the study, and who traveled from Boston to the New York hospitals for this purpose. The physician performed an independent review of the case and filled out a new adverse event form that replaced one or both of the other forms.

Missing charts in the individual hospitals evoked a good deal of concern. The study would have been greatly weakened if large numbers of records were not located: questions could be raised about whether a hospital had sequestered records that contained evidence of adverse events or substandard care. To ensure maximum cooperation, we conferred closely with hospital administrators before initiating the review in each institution. And we soon satisfied ourselves that the missing records were not concealing anything, but instead probably reflected the fact that record rooms are very busy, and records are often not readily found.

In fact, the cooperation and efficiency of the participating hospitals were remarkable: 30,121 of the 31,429 records selected for the study sample were produced on the first attempt. This 96 percent "locate" rate surpassed all our expectations. After the initial study ended we undertook a follow-up study involving a search for those records that were missing on our first visit. Adverse event and negligence rates were actually slightly lower in the missing records than they were in those records initially identified.[14] The fact that missing records were not concealing negligent cases provides further reason to believe that our record review results are representative and generalizable.

While the various methodological investigations attest to the accuracy of most of the study, other parts of our research indicated that many physicians tended to avoid attributing medical injury to negligence when judging standardized cases.[15] Reanalysis of our large data set also revealed the somewhat conservative nature of the negligence determinations. Thus, especially with regard to rates of negligent adverse events, our estimates are likely to be a lower bound.

Results

In our sample of 30,195 records we found a total of 1,278 adverse events that either occurred as a result of medical management during the index hospitalization (that is, the one under investigation) or that led to the hospitalization itself (Table 3.1).[16] Of this number, 306 injuries were the result of provider negligence. To calculate the incidence of adverse events, however, we limited our analyses to the 1,133 injuries that occurred or were discovered during the index hospitalization. For this purpose we eliminated those injuries that were discovered after discharge but did not require hospitalization (Category 2), as well as those in Category 3 that duplicated Category 5 (in Table 3.1). To investigate hospital-specific information, we used only the 922 injuries that we could positively identify as resulting from care provided at one of our hospitals. For risk factor analyses, we used all 1,278 events.

Table 3.1   Timing of adverse events and negligence

Category	Timing	Adverse events		Adverse events due to negligence	
		No.	%	No.	%
1	Occurred and discovered during index hospitalization	647	50.6	156	51.0
2	Occurred during index hospitalization, discovered during subsequent outpatient care	78	6.1	7	2.3
3	Occurred during index hospitalization, discovered during subsequent hospitalization	67	5.2	19	6.2
4	Occurred during outpatient care before, but discovered during, index hospitalization	167	13.1	59	19.3
5	Occurred during earlier hospitalization, but discovered during index hospitalization	319	25.0	65	21.2

RATES OF PATIENT INJURY AND PROVIDER NEGLIGENCE

Our results indicate that in New York in 1984 the incidence of adverse events suffered by hospitalized patients was 3.7 percent. Of these, 27.6 percent were due to negligence; that is, about 1 percent of all patients hospitalized suffered a negligent medical injury.

These figures are similar to those compiled in California more than a decade earlier. While the California study reported a somewhat lower negligence rate and a somewhat higher injury rate, the differences are not practically significant. Thus, these two large-scale and independent studies indicate that in approximately 4 percent of all hospitalizations adverse events take place, and one-quarter of these involve substandard care.

Our results are even more striking when the sample findings are weighted up to produce population estimates. Among the 2.6 million

Table 3.2   Disability caused by adverse events, based on 1984 New York State population estimates

Disability	Adverse events		Negligent adverse events		Adverse events due to negligence
	No.	%	No.	%	(%)
Minimal, recovery 1 month	56,042	57	12,428	46	22
Moderate, recovery 1–6 months	13,521	14	3,302	12	24
Moderate, recovery > 6 months	2,762	3	817	3	30
Permanent, 1–50% disability	3,807	4	869	3	23
Permanent, > 50% disability	2,550	3	877	3	34
Death	13,451	14	6,895	25	51
Not determinable	6,477	7	1,989	7	31
Total[a]	98,610	100	27,177	100	28

a. Totals differ from sums reported above because of rounding errors.

patients discharged from New York hospitals in 1984 we estimate that nearly 99,000 suffered disabling injuries (Table 3.2). Of these, 56,000 produced minimal impairment, from which the individuals recovered within one month. Another 13,500 led to moderate impairment, with recovery in less than six months. More than 70 percent of the adverse events we identified, then, led to reasonably short-term disability. Still, there were large numbers of individuals who suffered more serious injuries. More than 3,800 adverse events produced *permanent* impairment causing a level of disability ranging up to 50 percent, and another 2,500 patients suffered severe to total disabilities as a result of their treatment. Most dramatically, 13,400 New York patients died in 1984 as a result of medical treatment.

As in the California study, our results revealed a systematic relationship between negligence and the seriousness of the injury. Whereas only 23 percent of the impairments that lasted less than six months were the results of negligent treatment, 34 percent of the adverse events that led to permanent total disability were due to substandard care, as were 51 percent of the deaths from adverse events. Two-thirds of the injuries produced by grave negligence were fatal, six times the mortality rate from non-negligent iatrogenic injuries.

RISK FACTORS

These aggregate findings about the health care system are crucial for the broader medical malpractice debate, especially when connected to the data presented in the next chapter from our analysis of malpractice litigation records. In order to reduce the medical injury rate, both through public policies and through measures adopted within the health care system itself, it is even more important to identify factors that affect injury rates. In this work we use both univariate, or crude, and multivariate analyses. The latter methods allow us to examine the independent effect of one factor by using statistical techniques that control for the influence of other variables.

In what follows, we first consider which factors in the patient's situation may present a distinct risk of medical injury, and then do the same for individual characteristics of the hospitals. However, in the patient analyses we have controlled for place of hospitalization, since that may be a risk factor for an individual suffering an adverse event. In analyzing individual risk factors we used all 1,278 adverse events and the 306 adverse events we found to be due to negligence in the 30,195 records in the sample. Within this sample the mean adverse event rate was 4.2 percent, and the mean rate of adverse events produced by negligence was 26.7 percent.

Individual Characteristics   Whether using univariate or multivariate analyses, we found no difference in injury rate or negligence rate in the care given to men or to women. However, age was an important risk factor. Although individuals over the age of 65 constituted only 27 percent of the total number of hospitalized patients, they suffered 43 percent of the adverse events and 52 percent of the negligent adverse events. This additional risk to the elderly persisted even after we standardized for the severity of the illness. Thus, although their higher injury rates can be attributed in part to the frail physical state

Table 3.3   Univariate analysis of adverse events and negligence: effects of race, income, insurance status for patients less than 65 years of age

Variable	Adverse event rate, standardized % (SE)	Adverse events due to negligence % (SE)
Race		
Black	5.4 (0.8)	36.0 (5.2)[a]
White/others	4.0 (0.3)	23.6 (2.0)
Income		
< $10,609	5.7 (0.7)[b]	36.5 (4.8)
$10,609–15,904	4.3 (0.5)	24.9 (5.1)
$15,095–21,113	3.1 (0.3)	24.0 (3.3)
$21,114–31,724	4.3 (0.3)	24.7 (3.2)
> $31,724	4.1 (0.4)	25.3 (4.6)
Insurance		
Self-pay	2.9 (0.4)	40.3 (6.9)[c]
Medicaid	4.1 (0.5)	29.1 (5.3)
Private	3.0 (0.2)	20.3 (2.1)

a. $p < 0.05$ compared with white.
b. $p < 0.05$ compared with individuals with income > $10,609.
c. $p < 0.05$ compared with Medicaid and private insurance.
Note: SE = standard error.

of older patients, the higher negligent injury rates may also be a result of the quality of care the elderly receive from health care providers.[17]

Equally obvious was the disparity in the quality and risk of care according to race and economic status (Table 3.3). In univariate analyses, several socioeconomic factors appeared to be risk factors for medical injury and substandard hospital care. For example, the percentage of adverse events due to negligence was significantly higher among blacks than among whites and patients of other races.

Income levels, estimated by median household income by ZIP code, were related to both adverse event and negligence rates. Patients below the poverty level (less than $10,609) suffered significantly higher adverse event and negligence rates than all other income groups.

Payor status was not associated with significant differences in adverse event rates. Restricting the analysis to patients under 65 years of age, we found that self-pay (uninsured) patients had an adverse event rate of 2.9 percent, compared with 4.1 percent for Medicaid patients and 3.0 percent for privately insured patients. On the other hand, self-pay patients suffered significantly greater negligence (40.3 percent) than both Medicaid patients (29.1 percent) and the privately insured (20.3 percent).[18]

In order to examine comprehensively the effect of individual socioeconomic factors on the rates of adverse events and negligence, we performed multivariate analyses that included all characteristics specific to the patient and to the hospital to which the patient was admitted (Tables 3.4 and 3.5). When we included all such characteristics (along with the Diagnosis Related Group [DRG] category,[19] which controlled for severity of illness),[20] we found that age and Medicaid status were significant determinants of adverse events. Patients 45–64 and over 65 had significantly higher injury rates than did younger patients. Similarly, Medicaid patients had significantly higher injury rates than did younger patients or other payor groups. Patient race, income, and gender were not, however, associated with variations in the rate of iatrogenic injury.

The multivariate analyses also revealed that patients over 65 years of age were at increased risk of receiving negligent care than were younger patients. Self-pay patients were also at greater risk of negligence. However, the association of race and low income with negligent care that appeared in the univariate analysis disappeared when we controlled for other patient variables.[21] Thus, patient age and lack of health insurance (at least commercial or government insurance), not race and income, turned out to be the major risk factors for receiving poor quality care.

Hospital Characteristics   When we examined the characteristics of the hospital we found great disparities in both adverse events and negligence from one hospital to another. The medical injury rates varied from 0.2 to 7.9 percent, with an average rate of 3.2 percent. The percentage of adverse events due to negligence for all hospitals was 24.9 percent but across different hospitals ranged from as low as 1 percent to as high as 60 percent. These large and statistically significant variations in negligence from hospital to hospital signal that

Table 3.4   Multivariate analysis of individual-level risk factors: adverse event rates

Variable	Beta coefficient	Odds ratio[a] (95% confidence interval)	p value
Male gender	−0.04	0.96 (0.83–1.10)	NS
Black race	0.12	1.13 (0.84–1.51)	NS
Age group (omitted category: 16–44 years)			
Newborn	−1.57	0.21 (0.14–0.31)	<.05
0–15 years	−0.25	0.78 (0.56–1.08)	NS
45–64 years	0.55	1.73 (1.50–1.99)	<.05
> 65 years	0.79	2.20 (1.75–2.77)	<.01
Payor status (omitted category: private insurance)			
Self-pay	−0.18	0.84 (0.59–1.18)	NS
Medicaid	0.24	1.27 (0.97–1.65)	<.10
Income (omitted category: higher income)			
Poor	0.14	1.15 (0.90–1.46)	NS
Near poor	−0.09	0.91 (0.67–1.24)	NS
Low income	−0.44	0.64 (0.49–0.84)	<.05
Middle income	0.06	0.94 (0.79–1.12)	NS
DRG level (omitted category: DRG 2)			
DRG 1	−0.23	0.79 (0.53–1.19)	NS
DRG 3	0.11	1.12 (0.93–1.33)	NS
DRG 4	0.50	1.64 (1.20–2.26)	<.01

Dependent variable: whether adverse event was negligent
Estimation method: logistic
Sample size: 30,121
Number of positive values: 1,278
  a. Calculated from multiple logistic regression.
  Note: NS = not significant.

substandard care was not randomly distributed. The group of hospitals in our study with the highest percentages of negligent adverse events had figures more than double the mean in the overall sample.

What hospital characteristics tended to influence the institution's place in the overall distribution? In univariate analyses, several hospital characteristics appeared to play an important role as determinants both of adverse event rates and of the percentage of those events due to negligence (Table 3.6). University teaching hospitals

Table 3.5   Multivariate analysis of individual-level risk factors: percentage of adverse events due to negligence

	Beta coefficient	Odds ratio[a] (95% confidence interval)	*p* value
Male gender	−0.14	0.84 (0.59–1.20)	NS
Black race	0.39	1.48 (0.80–2.75)	NS
Age group (omitted category: 16–44 years)			
Newborn	−0.41	0.67 (0.19–2.27)	NS
0–15 years	−0.47	0.62 (0.29–1.33)	NS
45–64 years	−0.21	0.81 (0.52–1.27)	NS
> 65	0.53	1.71 (1.08–2.71)	<.05
Payor status (omitted category: private insurance)			
Self-pay	0.85	2.35 (1.40–3.95)	.001
Medicaid	0.29	1.34 (0.70–2.55)	NS
Income (omitted category: higher income)			
Poor	0.21	1.18 (0.62–2.24)	NS
Near poor	−0.22	0.79 (0.34–1.84)	NS
Low income	−0.16	0.85 (0.41–1.75)	NS
Middle income	−0.01	0.97 (0.50–1.90)	NS
DRG level (omitted category: DRG 2)			
DRG 1	−0.39	0.67 (0.33–1.38)	NS
DRG 3	−0.24	0.79 (0.57–1.10)	NS
DRG 4	−0.31	0.73 (0.41–1.30)	NS

Dependent variable: whether adverse event was negligent
Estimation method: logistic
Sample size: 1,278
Number of positive values: 306
   a. Calculated from multiple logistic regression.
   Note: NS = not significant.

had a standardized adverse event rate of 4.1 percent, much higher than affiliate teaching centers and nonteaching hospitals. On the other hand, only 10.7 percent of adverse events at the university teaching hospitals were due to negligence. This combination of results is to be expected, because more of the patients in those institutions are very sick and thus less likely to tolerate additional trauma from treatment. Furthermore, their medical condition often leads to more numerous and more invasive procedures. The fact that large

Table 3.6 Univariate analysis of hospital factors associated with adverse events and negligence (%)[a]

Variable	Adverse event rate	Adverse events due to negligence
Teaching status		
Primary teaching	4.1	10.7
Affiliate teaching	3.4	30.1
Nonteaching	2.3	26.9
Ownership		
Proprietary	2.7	9.5
Governmental	2.7	35.7
Nonprofit	3.0	25.2
Location		
New York City	3.7	23.5
New York City suburbs	2.4	35.0
Upstate MSA[b]	2.8	24.0
Upstate non-MSA	1.0	23.6
Proportion minority discharges		
>80%	3.7	37.0
15–79%	2.9	33.4
>15%	2.8	21.1
Number discharges		
<8,000	2.3	24.9
8,000–19,999	3.2	26.3
>19,999	2.9	24.5

a. Crude rates are univariate analyses that have not been modified for the effects of other factors with regression equations.

b. MSA = Metropolitan Statistical Area.

size of the hospital (defined as more than 19,999 patient discharges per year) was associated with lower adverse event rates (in our multivariate analyses) further supports the importance of teaching status, independent of hospital size. On the other hand, given the commitment to advanced methods and the higher degree of oversight available in university teaching programs, one would expect to find in teaching institutions lower proportions of substandard care among the medical injuries that did occur. This also turned out to be the case.

The ownership status of the hospital was not correlated with ad-

Table 3.7   Multivariate analysis of significant risk factors for adverse events

Variable	Beta coefficient	p value
Teaching status (omitted: nonteaching)		
Affiliate teaching	.42	.087
Primary teaching	.83	.023
Size (omitted: medium)		
Small	−0.24	.249
Large	−0.46	.043
Location (omitted: upstate urban)		
Rural	−0.88	.0002
New York City suburbs	0.00	.985
New York City	0.191	.491

Dependent variable: whether adverse event was negligent
Estimation method: logistic
Sample size: 30,121
Number of positive values: 922

verse event rates. The percentage of adverse events attributable to negligence, however, was much lower in proprietary hospitals (9.5 percent) than in nonprofit or government hospitals. Moreover, more than 35 percent of adverse events were due to negligence in government hospitals. On the other hand, the location of hospitals also appeared to be correlated with variations in iatrogenic injury, but not with quality of care. New York City hospitals had a high adverse event rate (3.7 percent), while rural hospitals had an adverse event rate of only 1.0 percent. With regard to negligence, the differences between regions were not statistically significant.

Hospitals with more than 80 percent minority discharges had adverse event rates of 3.7 percent, which was higher than in predominantly white hospitals, but not significantly so. However, negligent adverse event rates were significantly higher in the largely minority hospitals (37.0 percent) than in others.

In order to examine the relationships among hospital factors while controlling for the individual risk factors of age and severity of illness, we completed multiple logistic regression analyses (Tables 3.7 and 3.8). Many of the relationships that emerged from the univariate

Table 3.8   Multivariate analysis of significant risk factors for negligence

Variable	Beta coefficient	p value
Teaching status (omitted: nonteaching)		
Affiliate teaching	−0.08	.811
Primary teaching	−1.36	.018
Ownership (omitted: nonprofit)		
Public	−0.08	.831
For profit	−1.35	.004
Racial mix (omitted: predominantly white)		
Mixed race	0.48	.088
Predominantly minority	0.86	.032

Dependent variable: whether adverse event was negligent
Estimation method: logistic
Sample size: 922
Number of positive values: 190

analyses were maintained when other factors were controlled. When all hospital characteristics were included, along with patient age and the DRG category to control for severity of illness, three attributes were revealed to be significantly associated with the risk of medical injury. University teaching hospitals had a higher rate of adverse events than did voluntary nonteaching hospitals. Hospitals in upstate, rural locations had fewer adverse events. Finally, large hospitals had fewer adverse events than medium-sized ones.

The only factor significantly associated with an increased proportion of medical injury due to negligence was a high proportion of minority discharges. Significantly lower percentages of negligence occurred in university teaching hospitals and in proprietary hospitals. It appears, then, that factors associated with hospitals located in poor minority communities are important determinants of the quality of care rendered their patients.

Treatment Characteristics   We next computed injury rates for different medical specialties, using a Diagnostic Related Groups methodology. For instance, all the various DRGs for cardiothoracic surgery (such as coronary artery bypass grafts or aneurysm repair) were grouped in one category. We found a 32-fold variation in iatrogenic injury rates, ranging from 0.5 percent in the treatment of newborns by pediatricians to 16.1 percent in patients undergoing vascular surgery. Cardiac surgery (10.8 percent) had three times the adverse event rate of general medicine (3.6 percent). These injury rate differences were highly significant statistically. However, no significant differences were found in the negligence ratios from one specialty to another: for example, 18 percent and 23 percent respectively of the adverse events in vascular and cardiac surgery were negligent, as compared with 26 percent and 31 percent respectively in the newborn and general medicine cases. This means that although the total number of negligent injuries inflicted by surgeons was higher than the number of injuries caused by internists, for example, the difference appears to reflect the complexity and riskiness of the procedures performed by the two groups, and thence the very different consequences of momentary lapses by each.

Analyses of the sites of negligent adverse events produced information that will be useful to hospital risk management programs. For example, while only 3 percent of all adverse events occurred in the emergency room, fully 70 percent of those injuries were due to negligence. To some extent this very high negligence ratio stems from the fact that much of what is done in the emergency room is diagnostic in nature; consequently, the very definition of medical injury assumes some medical error. It also appears to reflect the fact that the emergency room, especially in poorly funded, big-city hospitals, is an extremely busy place in which doctors, nurses, and technicians are under great pressure to deal with heavy case loads. That pressure is conducive to the occurrence of negligent injuries to patients.

In examining types of adverse events and the subset attributable to negligence, we asked whether in particular clinical situations the patient was at higher risk of injury. Surgical treatment is often singled out when complications are mentioned, and surgical treatment did indeed account for the lion's share of adverse events in our study— 48 percent. But surgical adverse events as a group were less likely than nonsurgical ones to be judged negligent (17 percent versus 37 percent). Similarly, technical errors related to performance of invasive but nonsurgical procedures (such as insertion of a chest tube, performance of cardiac catheterization, or insertion of a peritoneal dialysis catheter) were found to be due to negligence in only 15 percent of cases. On the other hand, surgical adverse events that reflected failure to achieve attainable goals, such as a pregnancy after tubal ligation or a second operation after inadequate excision of a lumbar disc, were more likely to be attributed to negligence (36 percent). Our sample size did not permit computation of meaningful percentages for negligence associated with other types of adverse events, such as those related to anesthesia, falls, fractures, or neonatal or postpartum care.

Diagnostic errors accounted for only 8 percent of total adverse events, but 75 percent of these were judged to be the result of negligence. Further, the chance of serious traumatic outcome (as revealed in the medical records) was greater in patients with diagnostic adverse events: 47 percent died or suffered permanent disability. Of the nonsurgical, non-medication-related therapeutic adverse events, 77 percent were found to be due to negligence, and 35 percent were associated with a high degree of serious disability.

Of the nonsurgical adverse events, those related to medications were most common, accounting for 19 percent of all adverse events. Given the multitude of drugs administered to most hospitalized patients (on average patients received 10 different kinds of drugs), it is not surprising that drug-related injuries were frequent. Although most drug-related adverse events were relatively minor, 14 percent resulted in permanent disability or death. Medication injuries were also less likely to be due to negligence than almost any other. One reason is that a substantial fraction of such adverse results, those due to unpredictable side effects or allergic reactions, are not preventable given the current state of medical knowledge. Another leading subgroup of drug-related adverse events was (predictable) side effects of chemotherapy for cancer, a context in which patients willingly accept what is often a high risk of complications in the hope that their disease will be controlled.

The structured AEAF required that our physician reviewers assess whether an adverse event was possibly due to an error in management before making a judgment of negligence. In 58 percent of cases a potential error was identified, but only half of these were ultimately judged to be negligent. Almost all the adverse event determinations were clear-cut cause or no-cause verdicts, with only a small fraction (just over 5 percent) being close calls (i.e., scores of 3 or 4). In contrast, judgments about negligence tended to be distributed more evenly across the confidence spectrum, with a significantly higher proportion (18 percent) of close-call cases.[22] That finding was in line with what both our pilot studies and our physician surveys revealed concerning the difficulties doctors have in making judgments about negligent care, and the even greater problem of securing agreement from different doctors on this subject.

Implications

Several findings from this study are worthy of emphasis. First is disclosure of the overall magnitude of mortality and morbidity produced by iatrogenic injury. In New York in 1984 almost 100,000 injuries occurred as a result of adverse events, and more than a quarter of those were caused by substandard care. These numbers are even more striking when compared with other important sources of accidents in this country. This is especially true of the fatality rate. If New York's adverse-event-related death total can be extrapolated to the U.S. population as a whole, one would estimate over 150,000 iatrogenic fatalities annually, more than half of which are due to negligence. Medical injury, then, accounts for more deaths than all other types of accidents combined, and dwarfs the mortality rates associated with motor vehicle accidents (50,000 deaths per year) and occupation-related mishaps (6,000 deaths per year).[23]

We caution, however, against too quick a comparison of such fatality figures. In our study a death was judged to be iatrogenic if there was a clear causal link with medical management. But a substantial proportion of patients were gravely ill, and many would have died from their underlying illnesses in months, days, perhaps hours, even absent the mishap in treatment.

Consider the following example. A patient suffering from advanced lung cancer and an infection had severe breathing impairment and was placed on a respirator. The respirator overinflated the lungs, causing them to ride up higher in the chest. Because the patient's blood pressure fell, he needed special medication which was (properly) given through a catheter into a large vein in the uppermost part of the chest. Placement of the catheter led to laceration of the higher-riding lung, causing it to collapse (a condition called pneumothorax.) The unfortunate event was fatal for this very sick patient. We attributed the death to the pneumothorax caused by medical management: thus it was counted as an adverse event, even though the patient in question would probably have lived for only a few days at most before his underlying disease took its toll. Unfortunately, we cannot say what proportion of deaths from medical adverse events involved patients with relatively short life expectancies. We do know, however, that motor vehicle or workplace fatalities typically involve healthy individuals.

A better index of the riskiness of medical treatment was the number of permanent and total or near-total disabilities. Severe nonfatal injuries from medical management numbered 2,500 in New York State, which would be equivalent to more than 30,000 victims nationally, a total greatly in excess of comparable disabilities from the job, if not the road.

We found that medical injuries and negligence were not evenly distributed through the community, an observation in keeping with the findings of others. For example, blacks and members of other minority groups have been shown to receive fewer medical services and, some have suggested, lower quality care.[24] However, because blacks are more likely to be on Medicaid or to have no health insurance (that is, they are self-payors), any poorer quality care they receive might reflect their insurance status rather than their race. Indeed, studies have been done which suggest that uninsured individuals receive lower quality care.[25]

Our results suggest quite strongly that age and insurance status, not race or income, are the major determinants for negligent injury. Moreover, while age is also a risk factor for adverse events as such, insurance status is not (nor are other socioeconomic factors). Since negligent injuries are precisely the injuries that providers are best able to prevent, the fact that the uninsured are most exposed to this consequence of poorer quality care should weigh heavily in the ongoing debate about the financing of health care.[26]

The great variations in rates of patient injury and provider negligence from one hospital to another also have important policy implications. Government and other large third-party purchasers of health insurance have recently become more interested in the quality of the care that they purchase.[27] In some analyses, hospital-level factors appear to play an important role in determining the quality of care.[28] The trick is to measure quality. Some have focused on rates of readmission to hospitals as a sign of poor quality care.[29] Others are interested primarily in hospital mortality rates. For example, the federal government has generated and released information on mortality rates among Medicare patients in individual hospitals. That measure has been refined by health services researchers,[30] who have recently shown that for-profit and public hospitals have higher adjusted mortality rates than do not-for-profit hospitals.[31]

Interpreting such differences in mortality rates does, however, pose serious problems.[32] In particular, it has been argued that the Health Care Financing Administration's model for assessing mortality rates of hospitals does not adequately control for severity of illness.[33] The result is that good hospitals that care for large numbers of very sick people may inaccurately be classified as poor hospitals on the basis of their relative mortality rates. Others have reported that mortality rate differences are largely due to random variation.[34] For such reasons, many health care executives oppose even the publication of mortality rates,[35] asserting that if we really want to assess the quality of care, we need to move beyond the administratively easier comparisons of mortality figures to more-intensive review of patient records.[36]

Our adverse event rates do provide this essential information about the actual quality of care rendered in hospitals, because they reflect in-depth analyses of management rather than bare screening criteria. The Adverse Event Analysis Form led to an examination of outcomes. And the analysis itself forced our reviewers to go on to study the process of care and to provide a guided implicit judgment about the care rendered. Consequently, we consider it superior to outcome measures (such as mortality rates) alone.

By themselves, then, overall adverse event rates cannot tell the whole story. Indeed, the very reason that modern medical care is so risky is that the enterprise has become much more ambitious. Advances in science and technology have expanded the capacity of doctors to deal with growing numbers of medical problems for which no measures were previously effective. At the same time, many such medical interventions now involve intrusive and often hazardous procedures performed on patients whose physical condition makes them highly susceptible to harm.[37]

The judgment about provider negligence was thus crucial. After determining that a medical injury had occurred (a process-oriented outcome), the reviewer judged whether the care met the standard of a reasonable medical practitioner. This overt quality measure identified the subset of adverse events that were preventable. These should be the special focus of programs in quality assurance. The large variation in negligent injuries from one hospital to another indicates that some hospitals are delivering much higher quality care than are others. And the fact that disproportionate numbers of negligent injuries are inflicted on elderly and uninsured patients—that is, on victims who are less likely to be able to assert meaningful tort claims—is suggestive of the preventive value of malpractice litigation. We undertake an in-depth examination of this topic in the medical liability debate in Chapter 6.

Ideally, of course, our objective in quality assurance should be to prevent *all* medical injuries—particularly, but not exclusively, negligent injuries. Many of the non-negligent adverse events we identified were unavoidable given the current state of medical knowledge: an idiosyncratic drug reaction in a patient who had not previously taken the drug, or a postoperative myocardial infarction in a seemingly healthy patient. But all negligent adverse events are due to errors and so should be preventable. Reduction of the rate of patient injury will require that doctors and hospitals find more effective methods to reduce errors, and, perhaps even more important, that they develop fail-safe systems and procedures to minimize harm to patients resulting from inevitable human errors.

Finally, certain adverse events that are potentially preventable but cannot now be traced to an identifiable cause can be reduced or eliminated by adherence to more tightly crafted standards and procedures. Wound infections following surgery are a good example. Few such infections result from recognized contamination of an incision. However, the evidence indicates that maintenance of high standards of aseptic technique by every member of the operating team results in fewer infections than occur when doctors and nurses are less concerned about such protocols and procedures.

Prevention of medical injury is prominent on the agenda of our medical profession and our hospitals. Indeed, the safety and effectiveness of many current medical treatments stem from the development of techniques to reduce what were once considered nonnegligent adverse events. Examples include the high rates of heart block, bleeding, and mortality in the early years of heart surgery; a range of problems in the early days of organ transplantation; and the side effects of drugs that have since been modified. Research eventually revealed the source of errors that were originally considered unavoidable; the errors could then be reduced or eliminated through innovative safeguards.

There is ample evidence, then, that adverse events are a fruitful topic for study, particularly using the methodology of our hospital record review. Such a research program would depend heavily on systems analysis and would be followed by the development and dissemination of guidelines for practice. Because human errors will continue, particular emphasis must be placed on the development of automatic fail-safe systems, such as computerized systems that make it impossible to order or dispense a particular drug to patients with a known sensitivity to that drug. Later chapters will consider the contribution that can be made by either existing malpractice law or alternative forms of liability to the quest for better quality medical care.

CHAPTER 4

Patient Injury and Malpractice Litigation

Objectives

Hospital patients face a considerable chance of being hurt as a result of negligent treatment by doctors and other providers, and an even greater risk of injury from non-negligent medical intervention. The hospital record review highlights the urgent need for greater quality assurance efforts within the health care system; the review also provides an initial road map to where such investments in accident reduction would most likely bear fruit. We now turn to the dual role of the legal system in dealing with the medical injury problem: redressing the needs of patients who suffer disabilities, and motivating health care authorities to undertake measures to avoid such accidents in the future.

For an initial look at these issues we set out to learn exactly what was happening within the legal system. How many malpractice claims were being brought, and in what kinds of cases? Certainly most American doctors fervently believe that present-day malpractice litigation is excessive and erratic in its operation. Acting on that belief, physician associations have persuaded most state legislatures to enact legal obstacles to the filing of such patient suits: shorter and tighter statutes of limitations, procedures for claims screening and certification, restrictions on the size of contingent fees that patients can pay lawyers to take on the chancier cases. To assess the validity of these popular and political impressions we used the files of New York State's Department of Health to document the incidence and the distribution of malpractice litigation.

Actually, scholarly opinion has not been of the persuasion that there are too many malpractice claims. On the contrary, the medical setting has provided the strongest evidence that the real tort crisis may consist in *too few* claims.[1]

Frequently cited in support of this scholarly understanding is the work done by Patricia Danzon,[2] who followed up on the California Medical Association's *Medical Insurance Feasibility Study.*[3] Danzon compared the study's estimates of injuries taking place in California hospitals in 1974 with data collected by the National Association of Insurance Commissioners (NAIC) in its survey of malpractice claims closed from 1975 through 1978 in California and elsewhere across the nation. Danzon found that for every ten negligent adverse events—that is, instances of torts—actually occurring within the California health care system, only one malpractice claim was lodged in the California liability insurance system, even at the height of the crisis atmosphere in that state in the mid-1970s. And only 40 percent of such claims—that is, only 4 percent of the number of in-hospital torts—ever received any payment through the legal system.

As Danzon herself recognized, questions can be raised about this methodology. A large share of the NAIC sample—claims closed from 1975 through 1978—actually stemmed from pre-1974 hospitalizations. It is fair to assume, though, that this disjunction in timing would not seriously affect the claims-to-injury ratio, because the 1974 medical injury rate uncovered in California was probably much the same as it had been in the earlier years, and the findings presented in Chapter 3 from New York a decade later corroborate this expectation. However, the total number of tort claims was probably somewhat higher than indicated in the NAIC study, which relied on voluntary reports from commercial insurers in California, and thus presented a somewhat incomplete measure of total claims. Omitted, in particular, was the claims experience of such large public, self-insured institutions as the University of California teaching hospitals and physician staff.

More important, the present malpractice system is operating at a much higher level than it was in the mid-1970s. Standard measures of claims filed per doctor more than doubled nationally from the mid-1970s to the mid-1980s, leading Danzon herself to estimate the present ratio to be on the order of 1 claim per 5 negligent medical injuries, rather than 1 per 10.[4] And since bodies such as the U.S.

General Accounting Office (GAO)[5] had reported medical malpractice claims rates in New York that were the highest in the nation—1 claim each year for every 3 practicing physicians in the state—the implication was that the medical injury/tort claims gap would be far smaller in the mid-1980s in New York than it had been in the mid-1970s in California.

That, in any event, was our expectation when we embarked on our malpractice litigation analysis. In contrast to the California work, our study had the advantages of both statistically valid population estimates of iatrogenic injury and a state law enacted in 1975 that required liability insurers to report all malpractice claims to a central repository, the Office of Professional Medical Conduct (OPMC) in the Department of Health.[6] With these resources, we would be able to pin down a precise measure of the injury/claims ratio.

But we recognized that such an approach would produce only an aggregate ratio, that is, a comparison of the total number of negligent adverse events with the total number of malpractice claims filed for the relevant year. The true risk that a negligent adverse event will produce a malpractice claim (according to Danzon, in California that risk was at most 10 percent in the mid-1970s and 5 percent in the mid-1980s) can be measured only under the tacit assumption that all the claims filed reflect negligent injuries actually suffered (even if nowhere nearly all the injuries suffered do generate filed claims). Yet on reflection that assumption is unlikely to be entirely valid. The very inability of so many patients to connect their present disability to past medical maltreatment[7] and then persuade a lawyer that prospects of success are good enough to warrant suit also makes it likely that many patients and lawyers will mistakenly make such a connection and will file suits even if the patient was not really the victim of medical negligence.

As a second major feature of our litigation review, then, we set out to test these assumptions directly by documenting which malpractice claims were valid and which were not. We did so by matching our judgments from the medical record review about which patients had legitimate tort claims, with our litigation data about which patients actually filed claims.

The immediate objective of that investigation was to determine whether the litigation system was reasonably accurate or was quite erratic in targeting true cases of provider negligence and patient injury. If there was considerable inaccuracy in the tort selection process, such that some malpractice claims were filed even though negligent adverse events had not occurred, the aggregate injury/ claims ratio derived from the earlier phase of the litigation review would in fact understate the true litigation gap. In other words, for every claim we found that was not matched to a negligent adverse event, another negligent adverse event would not have produced a malpractice claim to be incorporated in the aggregate claims total.

Methods

CLAIMS REPORTS

Crucial to the validity of the results from our litigation review was a complete collection of all malpractice claims filed in New York. Unfortunately, when we first investigated the claims records, we quickly learned that compliance with the 1975 malpractice claims reporting requirement had been spotty. Not only was the data base generally incomplete, but the gaps were distributed erratically, affecting certain carriers and self-insurers much more than others.

Our project, however, served as a stimulus to the state's Departments of Health and Insurance to enforce much more strictly the claims reporting and certification requirement. The results of these efforts, which began in late 1987, were quickly visible. Whereas in each of the six quarters prior to the end of 1987 the OPMC had received about 2,500 reported claims, in the next three quarters that figure increased to 4,300. The additional reports even included some from the New York Liquidation Bureau, an agency that manages claims covered by insolvent insurers. Of two large self-insurers that encountered logistical difficulties in reporting to the OPMC using the latter's format, one sent us more than 500 hard-copy claims reports to keypunch, and the other allowed members of our study team personally to inspect and extract data from over 1,400 claims files on site. The result was that by the summer of 1989, when we began our analysis, we had a data base of just under 68,000 claims that had been filed from 1975 until early in 1989.

We are satisfied that this effort gave us a comprehensive record of all malpractice claims initiated in New York during that period, which we could then compare with the number of negligent injuries that occurred during 1984 hospitalizations. There was a potential gap in the claims file, though, involving possible claims from 1984 hospitalizations that had not yet been filed. We had deliberately selected 1984 as a year that was early enough to minimize this problem, given the statutory limitation period of 2.5 years. However, there is sufficient sponginess in the legal definition of this period (for example, that the filing time does not begin to run until after the end of the period of "continuous" treatment) to permit a not insignificant number of cases to be filed some years later. Indeed, our own analysis of the claims filed from 1975 onward indicated that approximately 10 percent of malpractice claims are filed more than four years after the date of the medical accident, and 7 percent after five years. However, by the summer of 1989 5.5 years had elapsed from hospitalizations during January 1984, and 4.5 years from hospitalizations during December 1984. In addition, a sizable proportion of the negligent injuries we had identified stemmed from medical errors that manifested themselves in the records of 1984 hospitalizations. Thus, we expect that no more than 5 percent of claims from 1984 hospital accidents were yet to be filed.

For this reason, and also because there is some difficulty in identifying the actual medical accident date from a claims report, we used an alternative method to cross-check our initial estimates based on claims reported for the 1984 accident year. The alternative estimate was based on the annual average number of claims opened in the years 1984 through 1986: we assumed that the total number of claims filed in one malpractice *litigation* year that arose from a number of prior medical accident years should roughly correspond to the total number of claims based on one *accident* year, but filed in a number of later litigation years.

DEFINITION OF CLAIMS

Gaps in collected claims files are not, however, the principal source of the huge variation in reported rates of malpractice (or other tort) litigation. With respect to New York, for example, the GAO, in its six-state study issued in early 1987, asserted that there were 36 claims per 100 physicians in New York in 1984.[8] In early 1988, New York's own Insurance Department report stated that there were 9 *paid* claims per 100 physicians in 1984,[9] a result which implies that fewer than 20 claims were *made* per 100 physicians (given that nearly 50 percent of patient claims are successful). The major reason for such disparities is variation in the definitions of "claim."

To avoid such ambiguities we adopted the following specifications for the concept of "claim" that was most appropriate for our purposes.

- A malpractice *claim* is broader than a legal *suit* filed as the first step in formal litigation. It is not unusual for a patient's claim to be lodged with and settled by the insurer and/or provider without any formal legal steps being taken, indeed without the patient's even using a lawyer.
- Insurers, however, often calculate and report *potential* tort claims that are different from and usually larger than the number of *actual* claims. To establish adequate reserves, insurers take account first of "observational" claims regarding incidents perceived by an insured on the scene as troublesome and likely to generate a later claim, and second, "incurred but not reported" (IBNR) claims based on actuarial projections of where the aggregate claims trend seems to be heading. For our purposes, though, we utilized only those malpractice claims that had actually been filed by patients, not claims that doctors or actuaries had predicted (perhaps mistakenly) might be filed.
- Finally, a single *patient* claim may involve a number of *provider* claims. For evident reasons, a patient seeking legal redress may file several claims against different physicians and/or institutions involved in the treatment. Reporting the rate of provider claims is the aptest way to assess the size of the litigation burden and deterrent threat experienced by doctors. However, for our purposes—determining to what extent there is a gap between the number of negligent adverse injuries inflicted on patients and the number of tort claims filed by patients as a result of these injuries—the relevant figure is the somewhat smaller total of patient claims. (From our review of the OPMC data file, it turned

out that there were 1.5 provider claims for every one patient claim.)

CLAIMS MATCHES

Assembling the entire pool of malpractice claims (as defined above) enabled us to compare the total number of patient claims arising from 1984 hospitalizations and the total negligent injuries to patients identified by our review of hospital records for that year. But that aggregate assessment of the claims gap was deficient for the reasons stated earlier: to refine this assessment further we needed to document those claims filed by patients that were valid and those that were not (on the basis of our independent judgment from the hospital record review).

Unfortunately we were not able to undertake this comparison in the easiest fashion, by asking each of our patients whether or not he or she had filed a claim. Although we located and interviewed the patients whom we had determined were the victims of iatrogenic injuries, the one question our participating hospitals had enjoined us *not* to ask was whether the patient had filed suit as a result of hospitalization (for fear the question itself might precipitate a lawsuit).

Therefore, we undertook an elaborate matching procedure between the OPMC claims data and the hospital records.[10] From a variety of identifiers in both data files we first determined how many of our patients had lodged claims. An experienced medical-legal team then read the material in both the claims synopsis and the hospital record to determine which of the patient claims arose out of or were related to care provided in our sample hospitalizations. Using the sample rates for each case thus identified, we were then able to project the total number of claims filed by the entire population of 1984 patients. This procedure gave us a third cross-check on the aggregate estimates arrived at from the OPMC's entire claims file. More important, identification and subtraction of the claims filed without positive evidence in the hospital file of a negligent injury enabled us to calculate the true odds that a patient who was actually the victim of a tort in the hospital would lodge a tort claim against the provider.

Results

MALPRACTICE TRENDS

The following trends in malpractice litigation in New York emerged from the comprehensive data file assembled in the Department of Health for our study:[11]

- Despite the supposed statutory limitation of 2.5 years for filing a malpractice claim, about 10 percent of such claims were filed later than 4 years after the original accident date.
- The tail of claims *disposition* was even longer than it was for claims *filing*. Fifty percent of claims were closed more than 5.5 years after the date of the medical accident, 25 percent more than 7.5 years later, and 10 percent more than 10 years later.
- The frequency of claims arising out of any one accident year rose steadily, from 3,200 claims in 1976 to 5,400 in 1984. However, the increase was slower with respect to claims filed against individual physicians—rising from 2,300 to 3,200—because the physician (as opposed to the institutional) share of all malpractice claims was dropping from 71 percent to 59 percent in the state.
- In a significant proportion of cases, several providers (one or more doctors and the hospital) were the targets of malpractice claims generated by the same medical accident. Overall, there were 1.5 claims against providers for every 1 claim by a patient. The flip side of that coin is that claim success was greater for patient claims than for provider claims: whereas just over 40 percent of providers against whom claims were filed had to make a payment of some kind, 50 percent of the patient-claimants collected some money for their injuries.
- The amounts paid on claims—that is, claims severity—rose quite sharply in the state. Payments made by providers on closed claims rose more than fivefold from 1976 to 1988: from $28,000 to $158,000 in *average* payments, and from $8,500 to $59,000 in *median* payments. With inflation controlled for, the real value of these provider payments roughly trebled in this twelve-year period. And since amounts received by successful patients had to be roughly 50 percent greater than the payments made by providers (there were 1.5 provider-defendants for each patient-plaintiff), the

average successful patient was collecting approximately $225,000 in damages by 1988.

- On the other hand, claims frequency has not risen as steeply as depicted by the GAO report, for example, which stated that claims per 100 physicians in the state rose from 27 in 1980 to 36 in 1984.[12] Using all physicians as the denominator for this ratio, we found that claims rose from 6 per 100 physicians for the 1976 accident year to 7 per 100 for 1984. It is true that the total physician population includes a large number of doctors engaged in teaching, research, administration, and other activities which involve only a slight probability of personal suit. Yet when we examined data from the state's two largest physician insurers, whose policyholders were engaged in active medical practice and thus exposed to malpractice claims, we found that their frequency rate rose from 11 claims per 100 physicians in the 1976 accident year to 13 per 100 for 1984.

MALPRACTICE GAP

Of course, viewed from almost any other perspective than the GAO's grossly inflated estimate, the statistical prospect that 1 out of 8 doctors will be sued personally every year strikes most people as highly burdensome. But the question is how this slowly but steadily rising litigation rate against doctors compares with the rate of negligent injuries being inflicted by the health care system on patients—that is, with the potential number of malpractice claims that could be brought. The answer is to be found in Table 4.1.

The first estimate in this table simply totals all the patient claims in the OPMC file for the accident year 1984 and compares this total with our population estimate of negligent patient injuries for that year. The second estimate averages on an annual basis all the claims filed in the litigation years 1984 through 1986 and then makes a similar aggregate comparison. Both procedures produced essentially the same result: slightly more than 7 patients suffered a negligent adverse event for every patient who filed a tort claim. Although the likelihood of suit is somewhat greater than the 10-to-1 ratio estimated for California in the mid-1970s, it is significantly smaller than the less than 5-to-1 ratio we expected for New York in the mid-1980s.

Table 4.1   Negligent injuries and patient claims, New York State, 1984

Data basis	Number of claims	Negligent injuries	Ratio of negligent injuries to no. of claims
Claims for accident year 1984, OPMC file	3,782	27,179	7.2
Average annual claims opened 1984–1986, OPMC file	3,672	27,179	7.4
Claims files 1984–1989 matching survey sample	3,571	27,179	7.6

The third estimate in the table is the product of our individualized matching procedure of claims to negligent injuries among the patients in our sample. We identified a total of 98 claims filed by our patients against 151 health care providers. (This 1.54 provider-patient claims ratio is almost identical with the 1.49 ratio we estimated from the entire OPMC data file.) Yet of these 98 claims, only 47 were positively linked to treatment given in the 1984 hospitalizations we had sampled. The sampling weights for the 47 cases produced a statewide population estimate of 3,571 patient claims for 1984 treatment—1 claim for every 7.6 negligent injuries we had estimated for that year from the medical record review.

One would not, of course, expect that every negligent adverse event—which we defined as including any disability lasting for at least a day—would produce a tort claim. The medical records indicated that most physical disabilities were modest and short-lived. Many of the more serious injuries or fatalities were inflicted on elderly patients, whose consequent financial losses would probably be comparatively low. Thus, nearly 80 percent (10,026 out of 12,859) of the patients who suffered a negligent injury but did not sue were either fully recovered from the injury within six months or were more than 70 years old when the injury occurred.

On the other hand, while the class of 2,833 nonlitigants under 70 with more serious injuries was small relative to the pool of older or seriously injured victims of medical negligence, the former group was numerous relative to the total number of malpractice claims filed. Recall that 3,782 malpractice claims were filed for the 1984 accident year, of which approximately half (or 1,891) would eventually produce some payment. Even with respect to these more "valuable" tort claims, then, the aggregate gap between potential and actual paid tort claims is approximately 5 to 2.[13]

MATCHING NEGLIGENT INJURIES AND MALPRACTICE CLAIMS

The foregoing aggregate ratios sharply understate the true litigation gap, because they assume that all claims made and paid were brought for true negligent injuries.[14] Yet the key finding of our detailed matching procedure was that in only 8 of the 47 claims filed by our patients as a result of their 1984 hospitalization was there an actual negligent adverse event in the treatment. As Table 4.2 shows, of the remainder, 10 claims involved hospitalization that had produced injuries, though not due to provider negligence; and another 3 cases exhibited some evidence of medical causation, but not enough to pass our probability threshold. That left 26 malpractice claims, more than half the total of 47 in our sample, which provided no evidence of medical injury, let alone medical negligence.

These observations do not imply that all the malpractice claims for which we were unable to detect a negligent injury in the hospital record will eventually prove ill-founded when investigation and litigation is complete. Close analysis of the cases that generated the apparent legal "false positives" indicates that a considerable number might well not have been identifiable through our procedure. For example, 12 of the 26 cases in which the hospital record displayed no evidence of even medical injury involved claims of a failure to diagnose a patient's condition during an ambulatory visit prior to hospitalization. In the 13 cases in which we found at least some evidence of medical causation, one of the two initial reviewing physicians found that negligent treatment had taken place. Because legal processing of these malpractice claims is not complete, we cannot presently tell how many of these claims will turn out to be valid or whether the legal system will dispose of the cases accordingly.

Yet the incomplete state of the record regarding what appeared to us to be unfounded malpractice claims does not affect the implication of this matching process for the size of the overall litigation gap. The

Table 4.2   Malpractice patient-claims in medical records sample

Subgroup	Discharges (sample)	Claimants (sample)	Estimated claimants (N.Y. population)	Claims per discharge	Comments
Cases not referred by MRA	22,378	12	889	0.045	5 cases allege failure to diagnose during ambulatory visit
Cases referred; possibility of AE	6,275	14	1,000	0.18	9 cases: M.D. knew about claim, found no AE; 4 cases: M.D. disagree, settled by review
Low-threshold AEs (less than likely)	335	3	92	0.30	1 case: 1 of 2 M.D.s found negligence
AEs more than likely; no negligence	853	10	561	0.79	6 cases: 1 of 2 M.D.s found negligence
AEs more than likely; negligence	280	8	415	1.53 (0, 3.24)[a]	1 case: review by only 1 M.D.
Totals	30,121	47	2,967	0.11 (.06, .16)[b]	

a. Based on population estimates of discharges. For example, 1.53% = 415/27,179.
b. 95 percent confidence intervals.
Note: MRA = medical record analyst; AE = adverse event.

reason is that for every one of the total number of malpractice claims that (rightly or wrongly) we judged to be unrelated to a negligent injury, we must subtract a claim from the total that was initially assumed to have been filed by the patient-victims of identifiable injuries. Specifically, in our hospital record review we found 280 negligent adverse events inflicted on our patient sample, and in our litigation record review we found 47 malpractice claims filed by our patients as a result of their hospitalization. It turned out, however, that only 8 of these claims were brought by the 280 negligent injury victims: this left a litigation gap of 272 rather than 233 (280 minus 47) cases. Expressed in the form of ratios calculated from the sampling weights, the chances that a claim would be filed by a patient with an identifiable negligent injury was not 1 in 7.6, but rather only 1 in 50.

Implications

We noted earlier that a common physicians' complaint about malpractice litigation is that it is both excessive and erratic. Our investigation of the incidence and distribution of litigation in New York demonstrates that while the legal system does in fact operate erratically, it hardly operates excessively. Indeed, precisely because so many claims brought by patients are misdirected, earlier comparisons of the totals of negligent injuries and malpractice claims actually disguised how small are the odds that a potentially legitimate tort claim will be brought.

The estimated 1-in-50 chance that a patient who suffers a negligent medical injury will file a malpractice claim overstates this gap somewhat. As of the date we cut off collection of claims data, there remained a few claims yet to be filed by patients for the 1984 hospitalization year. However, that number is so small—perhaps 5 percent of the 1984 total—that it is unlikely to make an appreciable difference in the overall claims gap, as evidenced by the close correspondence in the several estimates from the different procedures we used, presented in Table 4.1.

Potentially more significant was our inability to identify all the claims that were valid among those filed by the 47 patients in our sample. Such an undercount is inevitable when hospital records are used to detect negligence in a doctor's diagnostic or treatment decision made before the patient entered the hospital. But this inherent limitation in our record review procedure reduces not only our count of the number of valid *claims* filed by patient-victims of actual negligence—that is, the numerator in our ratio—but also the estimated number of negligent *injuries* suffered by patients in the entire sample—the denominator in our ratio. One might assume that the proportion of missed claims is somewhat greater than the proportion of missed injuries. However, there is unlikely to be a sufficient disparity between the two to make a dramatic difference in the overall negligence-to-claims ratio. At best this factor might raise the ratio as high as the upper limit of our current statistical confidence levels, putting the true tort gap at perhaps 1 in 30.

One reason for supposing that identification of only 8 valid claims out of the 47 claims filed by our patients constitutes an undercount is that approximately 50 percent of patients who bring malpractice claims receive some payment through litigation, paid for by approximately 40 percent of providers who are initially targeted for suit. We grant that using legal disposition as a benchmark for the proportion of valid tort claims would be regarded skeptically by most physicians, for it implies that the tort system operates with reasonable accuracy in resolving claims once they are filed by patients and their lawyers.

We were not able to judge the validity of that assumption from our own data, because most of our patient claims had not yet been resolved by the legal system when we undertook our analysis. However, two recent studies furnish useful evidence on this score. One looked at a large number of anesthesia claims closed across the country in the late 1970s and early 1980s.[15] The other examined claims arising from all forms of medical treatment that were filed against a single large medical center during the same period.[16] Both studies used as a "gold standard" independent medical appraisal of the validity of the legal claim, based on the entire claims file. The key findings of the two studies were in close accord. First, patients collected in approximately 90 percent of those cases that were judged by doctors to be valid; and second, although patients also collected on approximately 40 percent of claims judged to be unfounded, the payments made for the same types and severity of injury were far lower in the second situation than in the first.

One implication of these findings for our results is that the appropriate base of comparison for our two modes of investigation of the overall litigation gap is somewhere between the roughly 30-to-1 ratio of potential to actual claims *made*, derived from the individual matching procedure, and the 15-to-1 ratio of potential to actual claims *paid*, derived from a comparison of claims and injury totals (because almost all valid claims made will eventually be paid).[17]

On the other hand, it is clear that a substantial majority of malpractice claims that are filed by patients do not flow from true negligent injuries inflicted by doctors or other health care providers. Although the legal system appears to do a surprisingly accurate job of sifting out the valid from the invalid claims (in the latter cases paying the claimants nothing or just a small amount of damages), the fact is that many innocent doctors are subjected to unwarranted tort suits. Malpractice litigation appears, then, to be sending as confusing a signal as would our traffic laws if the police regularly gave out more tickets to drivers who go through green lights than to those who go through red lights. And as we shall see in Chapter 6, the financial and emotional burdens imposed on innocent doctors as they seek ultimate vindication against a groundless malpractice suit is far greater than that faced by innocent drivers who are given an unjustified traffic ticket.[18]

From this perspective, one can understand the appeal of legislative efforts to inhibit the filing of "false positive" claims against innocent doctors, for example by requiring, as a prelude to suit, medical certification of the validity of a malpractice claim or preliminary evaluation of the validity of a claim by an independent review panel.[19] But we must not lose sight of the impact that such legislative policies probably have on the litigation gap itself.

First, even given the difficulty that patients and their lawyers have in targeting malpractice claims in cases in which earlier negligent treatment caused a present medical disability, the legal system operates with considerably more accuracy than the bare numbers suggest. In particular, while the absolute number of unfounded claims is considerably larger than the absolute number of valid claims, the pattern depicted in Table 5.2 shows that the chances that any one doctor will be sued are far greater if negligent treatment has occurred than if it has not. To return to our traffic analogy, even though more drivers may be ticketed by police after going through green than red lights, the reason is that far more drivers go through green lights in the first place. With that difference controlled for, the odds that a careless driver will get a ticket, or that a careless doctor will be sued, are far greater than the odds faced by their careful counterparts. As we shall see in Chapter 6, however cloudy the malpractice signal might appear to doctors, both the reality and the perception of that signal have a pronounced tilt in the proper direction.

Experience with and research on medical review panels, for example, show that such procedures add little tangible improvement to the capacity of the litigation system to dispose appropriately of claims initially lodged by patients.[20] More important, legitimate concern about the "false positive" claims that plague innocent doctors who are sued must not disguise the far higher number of "false negatives" experienced by negligently injured patients who do not sue.[21] Our litigation study demonstrates a far greater gap than we had expected between tortious injuries inflicted on patients in hospitals and tort claims filed against health care providers. It is true that most of this tort gap consists of cases with modest physical injuries and financial losses. But even after controlling for this factor, we found several times as many seriously disabled patients who received no legal redress for their injury as innocent doctors who bore the burden of defending against unwarranted malpractice claims. Our data make clear, then, that the focus of legislative concern should be that the malpractice system is too inaccessible, rather than too accessible, to the victims of negligent medical treatment.

CHAPTER 5

Patient Losses and Compensation

Objectives

Given the large gap between the number of negligent medical injuries—that is, torts—occurring in the hospital and the number of malpractice claims being pursued in the legal system, it is natural to infer that there are too many iatrogenic injuries and too few malpractice suits. One should not, however, be too quick to draw that parallel between these apparent respective failings of the health care and the legal systems.

We would readily agree that infliction of a disabling injury on a patient in the course of medical treatment is an adverse event to be avoided if reasonably possible. It is not so clear, though, that the failure of the legal system to respond to every negligent injury is equally regrettable. The filing and processing of tort claims imposes a considerable burden on the parties involved as well as on the broader community. These immediate "harms" from use of the legal system should be borne, then, only if the imposition of tort liability produces sufficient social benefits to make the costs of liability worthwhile. This chapter and the next present the data necessary for such a comparative appraisal of the benefits and costs of malpractice litigation.

For those who consider that the purpose of tort law is to dispense corrective justice,[1] that judgment could be easily made from findings reported in the previous two chapters. The assumption of corrective justice is that when one party's faulty conduct (a doctor's carelessness) inflicts injury on an innocent victim (a patient), the role of the law is to restore the moral equilibrium by requiring the negligent actor to shoulder the burden of the victim's losses. From this per-spective every instance in which the tort system does not respond to a fault-caused injury constitutes an unacceptable failure to rectify a moral wrong. Contrariwise, when a tort claim is made—even worse, when such a claim is upheld—against an innocent actor, the legal harm thereby imposed on that actor is also intrinsically wrong. From either side, then, the data assembled through the reviews of hospital records and malpractice claims provide ample grounds for lamenting the performance of tort law.

Yet as we intimated in Chapter 2, the value of individualistic corrective justice as a guiding norm for medical liability is no longer very relevant in a world in which the burden of liability is distributed to the broader community through the interplay of malpractice in-surance and health care insurance. Instead, justification for using and constraining malpractice litigation must be found in a more pragmatic blend of sensible compensation, effective prevention, and economic administration of disabling injuries inflicted on patients. The important question this poses for our empirical investigation of the intersection of medical injuries and tort litigation is whether the need for tort compensation and/or the promise of tort prevention is so compelling that we should treat the paucity of malpractice claims as a problem (even granting the substantial administrative cost en-tailed by such litigation).

Systematic investigation of the compensation gap affecting injured patients was perhaps the principal objective of the study in New York. The finding from the California study in the mid-1970s, that only a small fraction of medical injuries ultimately produced a paid tort claim—a finding we have now replicated and refined for New York in the mid-1980s—had stood squarely in the way of serious consideration of fundamental alternatives to malpractice litigation, in particular the alternative of no-fault patient compensation. Since doctors and hospitals are already laboring under the burden of spi-raling premiums used to pay the mere handful of injured patients who are able to collect on their tort claims, it seemed unthinkable to entertain a proposal that would extend redress to the far greater total number of patients hurt by their encounters with the risky world of modern medicine.

The argument that no-fault insurance is unfeasibly expensive is not persuasive at the level of abstract social principle. However large the losses suffered by injured patients, however limited the compensation now provided by existing malpractice law, these real losses have to be borne—they must be "afforded"—by someone, either the immediate victim and family or the broader community. Indeed, a considerable share of such patient losses consists of the costs of treating iatrogenic injuries in the same health care system that accidentally inflicted the injuries in the first place. But whatever the moral merits or demerits of no-fault, understandable concern about the financial drain it would generate was a powerful stopper in the debate taking place within the political arena.

Yet it is not so obvious that this argument is valid even on its own terms. There is a marked difference between the occurrence of a physically impairing injury and a victim's subsequent experience of unredressed financial needs. For example, a patient's actual loss of earnings depends not so much on the mere occurrence of a iatrogenic injury as on the severity of the physical or psychological impairment caused by that injury, and on the functional disability the impairment then produces in the victim's performance of his or her usual job. Chapter 4 revealed that most iatrogenic injuries are relatively modest in dimensions, and that the graver impairments are considerably more likely to be caused by negligent treatment (and are thus at least potentially litigable). As a result, extending legal protection to non-negligent as well as to negligent medical injuries might not entail a disproportionate increase in financial expenditures.

To document the comparative cost of malpractice versus no-fault compensation we undertook the third major component of our study—an in-depth survey of the population of injured patients to determine the kinds of losses they subsequently experienced and the compensation, if any, that these patients received for their losses.

A good deal of earlier research had been done on the financial consequences of injuries in a variety of other contexts.[2] The consensus findings from this research were:

Most disabling injuries are short-term in character, and thus perhaps reasonably left to the victim's own resources.

The tort system tends to do a poor job of redressing the financial losses of the most severely injured victims.

But various systems of loss insurance do reimburse much of the cost of medical treatment and a significant share of the lost earnings of these victims (though a seriously inadequate share of earnings lost by the small number of long-term disabled victims).[3]

However, no such research had ever been undertaken on the patient-victims of medical accidents, even though such data are crucial to any informed policy judgment about the true compensation gap that is left by malpractice litigation, and thus about whether no-fault patient insurance is a financially viable option.

Guiding any such patient survey had to be some crucial policy judgments about the types of losses for which redress should be extended in such a compensation program. Within the malpractice system, historically rooted as it is in norms of corrective justice, it is estimated that nearly half of the compensation dollar is expended on compensating the successful claimants' pain and suffering.[4] However, when either malpractice litigation or a no-fault alternative is appraised as a mode of compensation, that distribution of the insurance dollar seems misplaced: at most only modest scheduled benefits would be paid for the nonfinancial losses stemming from iatrogenic injuries.[5]

Even with respect to financial losses, it makes sense to exclude the more numerous short-lived disabilities on the assumption that relatively modest losses are better handled through the victim's own private resources (including direct insurance arrangements such as sick leave), thereby obviating the administrative cost of processing a legal claim. The principal focus of such a no-fault program would be the longer-lasting disability that affects far fewer patient-victims but inflicts severe, even catastrophic, loss on the particular individuals and families concerned.

Making the longer-term disability the priority for no-fault insurance would have another major advantage in the medical context on account of a peculiar feature of iatrogenic injuries. Patients who see a physician or who enter a hospital are already disabled by their illness and are already experiencing costs of treatment and lost earnings as a result of their inability to work. Thus the injury that a patient may suffer during the hospitalization will prolong rather than initiate the disability in question. However, a no-fault program that is financed by and through the health care system should take responsibility only for the *additional* costs attributable to iatrogenic injury, not for the costs of illness attributable to general conditions of life in society. The problem, however, is that separating the costs attributable to the iatrogenic injury from the costs naturally arising from the background illness can be a difficult and expensive administrative task. A sensible demarcation line would limit payment of no-fault benefits to costs incurred by patients after a fixed time had elapsed, a time during which the disabling effects of most illnesses would probably have ceased. The time frame we initially felt would serve this administrative objective as well as the insurance priorities noted above was six months—the point at which New York's general temporary disability benefit plan ceases, and when social security disability benefits for permanent total disabilities have traditionally become available. However, in response to objections made against any such deductible period, we refined our data to depict the consequences of making benefits payable at any point from 0 to 6 months.

Another important issue in the design of a no-fault program, even with respect to the longer-term financial losses, is the relationship between the program and the other modes of community redress available to the patient. The no-fault medical accident programs in Sweden and Virginia, for example, are designed as secondary sources of compensation, thus complementing rather than replacing the broader, more easily administered medical and disability insurance provided by individuals, employers, or governments. Indeed, in a growing number of states, including New York, malpractice insurance has also been relegated to this backstop role by virtue of legislation that offsets against the tort damage award the benefits that have been received from collateral sources of loss insurance.[6] It was crucial, then, that we inquire of our patients not only what losses they had suffered but also how much of these losses (especially longer-term losses) had been paid for by alternative sources of compensation.

A final issue we must mention here—although it was not one we could directly appraise using our research findings—is the comparative administrative cost of no-fault versus tort-fault compensation.

Expenditures on claims administration—in particular, on legal fees —consume a large share of the claims dollar under any liability regime, fault or no-fault. Yet for reasons stated earlier, we could not ask our population of injured patients any questions about the legal fees they had incurred in either the tort system or in connection with other sources of injury compensation.

We do note that experience in other injury contexts leaves no doubt that a no-fault program such as workers' compensation has a much lower ratio of administrative to benefit costs than does the tort system, which is required to resolve highly contestable issues of fault.[7] However, the precise extent of this difference in any particular injury context is harder to pin down. Within the tort system, for example, medical malpractice is considerably more expensive to administer than motor vehicle litigation, because it is usually easier to determine the fault of a driver than the fault of a doctor. Tort litigation over airline crashes is even cheaper to administer because the liability of at least one defendant enterprise (airline, plane manufacturer, or air terminal) is assumed by everyone, and the only legal debate with the victim is over the appropriate amount of damages awardable. Similarly, in workers' compensation plans the cost of resolving workplace accident claims is much lower than the cost of occupational disease cases, because it is considerably harder to pin down the precise cause of a worker's cancer than the cause of loss of a limb. Numerous reports about the operation of no-fault patient compensation in Sweden and New Zealand[8] all indicate that there is far less legal conflict and administrative difficulty over claims administration in those systems than in present-day malpractice litigation in New York and elsewhere in this country. However, we cannot provide any precise estimates of the administrative savings from this factor.

Methods

The foregoing depicts the perspective from which we designed and conducted the patient survey.[9] Carrying out that survey was a major undertaking, both logistically and methodologically. What we had to do was locate and interview in 1989 a large sample of patients who had been hospitalized and injured in 1984 in order to generate the data from which we could make a statistically valid estimate of the total losses suffered by all New York patients from iatrogenic injuries that year. Those estimated losses had to include not only losses identified as having occurred between 1984 and the interview date, but also those projected to occur for the rest of the patients' lives.

SURVEY INSTRUMENT

We designed an elaborate survey instrument to gather all the information needed for our injury cost estimates. To help reduce potential errors in wording and logic, we utilized many questions from existing national survey instruments of economic losses. We asked all our respondents to specify what their primary activity was before their hospitalization: adult worker, homemaker, disabled, or retired, or child under the age of 16. Each respondent was asked questions about overall use of medical care and overall sources of income. Depending on their primary area of activity, patients were asked to complete the relevant sections of the survey instrument regarding their activities and losses between hospitalization and interview date.

The survey subdivided that time frame into six intervals, including the period before hospitalization, the hospitalization itself, and the period afterward. For each period we obtained and tabulated information about, for example, earnings of workers and income from a variety of nonwage sources (including social security, disability insurance, veterans' benefits, and a catchall "any other source"). Essentially the same procedure was followed with respect to the patients' use of health care services and ability to perform a variety of household tasks.

INTERVIEW PROCESS

Our sample for the survey consisted of 3,341 patients, comprising not simply people we had affirmatively judged to be the victims of medical injuries, but also patients whose medical records provided some evidence of causation (the "gray zone" cases), and a large number of matched control patients who had been hospitalized in 1984 but had not been injured at all.

Our experience with a pilot test of the patient survey had raised serious concerns about our ability to locate people who had been hospitalized five years earlier (especially in places like New York

City), and then to induce these people to submit themselves to an hour-long interview about their experiences since hospitalization (the vast majority of interviews were conducted by phone, although a few respondents without phones were interviewed in person), and then to have these patients recall the detailed information we needed for our financial projections.

Fortunately, we were able to locate nearly 90 percent of the original sample and to persuade nearly 90 percent of the eligible patients we had located to be interviewed. After excluding a number of respondents who did not satisfy our eligibility test, we were left with a respectable overall response rate of 70 percent.[10] Although extra efforts were made to locate and interview inner-city minority patients, the nonrespondents were most likely to be younger, minority, and covered by Medicaid. However, the initial sampling strategy enabled us to adjust for both noninterview cases and even for nonresponses to individual questions, so that our estimate of overall economic losses and compensation fairly represents the experience of the entire state population of injured patients.[11]

COST ASSUMPTIONS

To put individual responses into a common manageable format, we had to adopt a number of specifications for each of the categories of financial loss we were trying to estimate.

Medical and Rehabilitation Costs   Expenditures on medical care are notoriously difficult to determine from a personal interview. Most people do not know their health care costs, if only because the charges are usually paid by a health insurer. We therefore asked patients what services they had received, rather than what costs were paid on their behalf, then calculated the total cost figures by using average service prices derived from official sources. For hospital care we asked patients to recall when, where, and how long they had been in the hospital; we priced the hospital costs on the basis of average direct costs for that hospital in that year, using data from the New York Department of Health. A similar strategy was used for physician services for outpatient care, drawing upon annual surveys of physician fees; and for physical rehabilitation therapy and home health visits, relying on data from the New York Visiting Nurses

Association. To project the cost of future care, we first assumed that medical care utilization for the 1984 condition would have stabilized by 1988; then, using average costs incurred from 1986 to 1988 as the base, we projected that health care expenditure over the patient's own life expectancy would increase at an annual real rate of 5.5 percent (or slightly more than the actual medical inflation rate experienced in recent years).

Earnings Losses   To be able to calculate lost earnings from 1984 to the 1989 interview and thence project future losses, we first ascertained the period in which patients previously in the labor force were out of work for reasons associated with the 1984 hospitalization (as opposed to later layoffs, for example). For patients who had died or become permanently disabled as a result of their medical condition, we projected future time lost from work on the basis of national average work life expectancies for persons of the same age, race, and sex. Because these national averages refer to years of labor force participation, defined either as being employed or as actively seeking work, our results slightly overstate the duration of actual future work absences due to the medical condition.

Both for the survey period and for future losses we assumed that the patient's annual hours of work would have been the same as the usual hours prior to illness and/or the 1984 hospitalization. We valued those lost work hours at the pre-injury wage, inflated at an annual real rate of 0.7 percent, the observed rate of increase between 1985 and 1988.[12]

For the first time in such an injury survey, we also investigated the victims' loss of employer-paid fringe benefits, an increasingly significant component of employee compensation. For this purpose we used the cost to the employer of providing the relevant fringe benefit to workers in the industry in which they are employed; the average such cost is 16 percent of workers' wages.

In the case of permanently disabled or deceased children with no work history, we projected their lost earnings on the basis of average age-earning profiles. The data we used represent the average earnings of persons of labor force age, rather than the earnings of persons who are employed. By using these data, then, we implicitly assume that the future employment experience of these injured children would have been that of average persons of similar age and education.

Lost Household Production   In addition to its effect on employment, a disabling injury can limit the victim's ability to care for children, prepare meals, look after the home, and engage in the variety of other tasks of daily life. Lost household production is a tangible economic harm from a medical injury (as contrasted with the impact on recreational activities), and thus one whose costs we had to estimate through the survey.

As with lost time from employment, we first determined the number of weeks of household tasks that had been lost, initially between the 1984 hospitalization and the time of interview, and then, where relevant, as projected to the end of the patient's life expectancy. To minimize the length and burden of these interviews, the survey questions about lost household production were posed only to the women patients, both employed and nonemployed.[13]

We first asked each respondent to specify, for each of six household tasks, how often the task was performed in a typical week during the six months before hospitalization. The six tasks were child care, house cleaning, managing household finances, laundry, care of relatives, shopping, and cooking, which together account for the bulk of household work in the typical home. Rather than have our respondents try to recall exactly how much time they spent in these daily household activities, we used an earlier in-depth study conducted in Syracuse, New York,[14] of the time required for such tasks in families of different ages and sizes. Matching our patients' households to those in the Syracuse study enabled us to convert our patients' lost weeks of household production into lost hours per week, which were then multiplied by the estimated duration of the disability period.

We still had to translate the value of this economic loss into a dollar estimate of lost household production. There are two alternative methods for assigning a financial value to housework activity: replacement cost and opportunity cost.

The "replacement cost" method calculates the cost of buying the services needed to replace production of an injured or deceased homemaker. This method is very difficult to implement through anything but a detailed case-by-case analysis (the kind of analysis used, for example, in tort litigation), because of the problem of duplicating the manner in which people perform their household tasks. For example, although it might be possible to determine the average cost of having a child driven to school, or meals cooked for the family, or minor repairs done around the home, it is not feasible to add up these various costs in a manner that resembles how any particular homemaker would blend the several tasks together.

For that reason we used the alternative "opportunity cost" methodology, which, in effect, equates the value of an hour of household production to the amount that the homemaker could have earned by spending this hour in paid employment. Thus, if a woman was employed prior to her 1984 hospitalization, we valued her lost hours of household production at her hourly wage on the job. For women who were not employed outside the home, we estimated the amount they could probably have earned based on a comparison of their characteristics with those of women in the sample with wages from employment (the relevant characteristics being age, education, race, marital status, and geographic location.) We valued the lost hours of household production in each future year by assuming that real wages (actual or imputed) would increase at an annual rate of 0.7 percent, the same factor used earlier for estimating future lost earnings. We should note that not only does the opportunity cost method tend to overestimate actual financial losses from uninterrupted household production, but the projected lifetime costs of both wage and household production losses are overstated on a discounted basis to the degree that individuals vary in their actual dates of death. These costs are also overstated to some extent because the life expectancies of patients whose illnesses required hospitalization are probably shorter than the population averages we used for our estimates.

ADJUSTMENTS FOR NET COMPENSABLE LOSSES

Having calculated the projected lifetime losses suffered by our patient sample as the result of their 1984 hospitalization, we then had to tackle the most important and most difficult task of all—distinguishing the costs attributable to the medical injury itself from those that flowed naturally out of the original illness and the treatment it required. Before describing the methods we used for that purpose, we will briefly sketch some additional adjustments we then made in total accident costs to single out those losses that would otherwise be borne by the individual and that would therefore be appropriate candidates for a no-fault compensation scheme.

Personal Consumption Offset for Decedents   The death of a patient-victim presents this special problem for a compensation program: had the person survived, the decedent would have consumed part of the household income that had been earned—indeed, all of this income if there were no dependents. In computing the compensable losses to survivors, then, one must deduct the anticipated value of the decedent's own consumption of income.

Of the several admittedly imperfect methods for making such an estimate, we used the "equivalence scales" published by the U.S. Bureau of Labor Statistics.[15] These scales indicate what proportion of income one family needs in order to obtain the same level of welfare as another family, depending on the different ages, sizes, and composition of the two households. Applying these scales to the families in our patient sample enabled us to estimate the net loss in financial welfare suffered by a family from loss of a member who both earned and consumed income.

Income Taxes   For all patient-victims, income taxes constitute the most important wedge between the earnings previously received from employment and the net income lost to the worker and family. On the assumption that no-fault benefits would not be a form of taxable income, we used official tax scales and other data sources to calculate the amount of federal, state, and local taxes that would have been paid on the victim's projected earnings, and deducted this amount to arrive at a net compensable loss of income.

Other Sources of Compensation   Even in the absence of no-fault or tort compensation, the net income (as well as heath care) losses suffered by the patient are not necessarily borne by the individual victim and family. A variety of public and private loss insurance programs serve to distribute these costs across the broader society. For reasons stated earlier, we assumed that a no-fault program would serve as a second backstop payer to the more economical-to-administer regime of general loss insurance. That meant we had to identify all the benefit payments received from programs such as workers' compensation, social security, private disability and pension plans, and health insurance that were attributable to the hospitalization in question, and also to estimate the future receipts of such benefits in a manner analogous to our projection of future losses.[16]

With respect to sources of income reported by our patients, in a number of cases the new benefits received actually exceeded the prior earnings that had been lost. In those cases we simply set the net compensable loss figure at zero. As a result the ratio of benefits received to compensable losses within our entire group of patients is somewhat lower than the ratio of actual benefits to actual losses. With respect to medical insurance, given the great difficulty patients have in recalling precisely how much of their prior medical expenses were covered by insurance, our estimates of patients' compensable out-of-pocket costs were based on the national average for uninsured medical expenditures on various types of services during the several survey years. Finally, we did not include in-kind benefits such as food stamps or free medical care in our estimates of compensation payments received by our injured patients.

Discounting Future Payments   In calculating either the social or the individual costs of long-term disabilities, it is necessary to discount future compensatory payments down to a present capital value. Following the assumption that is now standard practice in tort law (but not yet in workers' compensation, for example), that injury victims should be protected from subsequent inflation, we used a real rather than nominal interest rate for this discounting purpose—assuming a 2.75 percent annual real return on long-term investments.[17] These present values were first discounted to the base year of 1984 and then inflated into 1989 dollars (using for the latter purpose the implicit gross national product deflator for personal consumption expenditures).

DISTINGUISHING MEDICAL INJURY COSTS FROM ILLNESS COSTS

We now turn to the problem mentioned earlier of disentangling the costs of medical injury from the costs of the underlying illness. Any patient who goes into a hospital to receive treatment for an illness is inevitably going to incur considerable health care costs on that account and will not be able to work in employment or in household production during the period of treatment and recuperation. In addition, many of the patients we studied had chronic degenerative diseases or conditions that would have been expected to cause severe disability or premature death irrespective of what happened in their treatment.[18] But the focus of no-fault medical injury compensation provided through the health care system itself must be on the financial consequences of untoward medical accidents, rather than on the consequences of the original ailments, which are attributable to the general human and social condition.

We employed two techniques for distinguishing the effects of iatrogenic injury from the effects of background illnesses to arrive at what we hoped would be mutually corroborative estimates of the true social costs of medical accidents. One method involved close physician analysis of the entire file for each of our injured patients—a file that consisted of the hospital record, the original physician review used to identify the adverse event, and the subsequent account of the patient's experience and condition derived from the patient or survivor interview five years later.[19] On the basis of all this material, our physicians—two doctors independently reviewing each patient file—decided which deaths and which episodes of health care use, or work or household disability, should be attributed to the original (or a subsequent) illness rather than to the medical injury discovered in our earlier hospital record review. The economists then assessed the financial cost of the periods of medical accident disability that had been identified in this way.

In effect, the foregoing analysis simulated the operation of a no-fault scheme that would operate on the basis of case-by-case analysis of the compensability of each patient's claim. In view of our instructions to physician reviewers to count as injury-related all spells of subsequent disability not clearly attributable to the illness, here also our results probably overstate the cost of medical accidents as such.

Because the microanalysis of each patient file did involve some individual case judgment, we utilized an alternative macroanalysis of the experience of the group of injured patients as a whole, comparing it with that of a control group of uninjured patients drawn from our sample.[20] Once the characteristics that would affect the likelihood of a disabling medical accident were thus standardized, the remaining differences in average losses between the two groups would represent the economic impact specifically attributable to medical accidents.

Two distinct methods were used to conduct these between-group comparisons. One method compared the experience of matched pairs of injured and noninjured patients. The matches were based on several characteristics: the patient's activity category (e.g., worker or homemaker), race, age, Medicaid or not, the hospital location, and the likelihood that a patient in this Diagnosis Related Group (DRG) would have a medical injury.

A second method, termed the "Oaxaca decomposition,"[21] whose results are reported here, did not require identification of individual matched pairs and so did not suffer from inevitable imprecision in the matching characteristics. We first specified duration of work or homemaking disability as a function of the patient characteristics noted above. The same equation was estimated for injured and control group patients respectively. We could then use differences in these estimated coefficients for the control and injured patient groups respectively to separate the amount of lost work or household production time that was attributable to the medical injury from lost time attributable to the background illness. The cost estimates presented here were obtained by multiplying the lost days attributed to the medical injury by the sample weights and average wages (or household time equivalents) for our injured patients.

This between-group method was workable for analyzing the loss of employment and household production time among adults, and thus served as a basis for comparison with results obtained for these losses from the case-by-case physician attribution technique described earlier. The sample of children was too small to permit between-group comparisons. In addition, between-group comparisons of medical care costs for either children or adults seemed inappropriate to us, because the costs of future care are eliminated for those patients who died: a higher proportion of deaths among injured patients would thus serve to reduce the estimated economic cost attributable to iatrogenic injury.

Results

Based on our interviews of the population-weighted sample, the following major findings regarding financial losses and compensation are calculated for New York's overall patient population in 1984.

AGGREGATE UNDISCOUNTED COSTS OF ILLNESS AND INJURY

We estimated that the lifetime undiscounted cost of both initial illness and iatrogenic injury for New York patients hospitalized in 1984 would amount to $21.4 billion. This figure comprises $2.6 billion in lost wages, $3.4 billion in lost household production, and $15.4 billion in medical care expenditures. Of these total costs, hospitalized children incurred only $1.1 billion, comprising nearly $175 million in future lost wages and $925 million in medical care expenditures.

DISTRIBUTION OF GROSS LOSSES

Of the workers who suffered adverse medical injuries, 94 percent were employed and 6 percent temporarily unemployed in the six-month period before hospitalization in 1984. Four percent of the workers died during hospitalization, and 6 percent died soon after discharge. An additional 15 percent of the workers who were alive at discharge never returned to work, three-quarters of these as a result of their ill health (for the others the reasons included caring for their families, going back to school, or inability to find a job).

Most of the injured employees and homemakers were able to return to their usual employment within a relatively short time (see Table 5.1 and Figures 5.1a and b). Thus, 63 percent of employees and 55 percent of homemakers resumed their usual tasks within six months of initial admission to the hospital. In line with a pattern that has been documented in other studies of workplace accident victims, the most severe economic consequences in our sample of medical accident victims were concentrated in a small segment of the population. As a result, more than 90 percent of the lifetime wage losses and 99 percent of the lifetime loss of household production were experienced by 21 percent of workers and 22 percent of homemakers respectively. Indeed, the largest component of total

Table 5.1   Distribution of injured adults' absences from work or household work[a]

| Duration | Work absences | | | Household absences[b] | | |
	Population	%	Cumulative %	Population	%	Cumulative %
1 month or less	9,595	34	34	17,713	33	33
2 months	3,411	12	46	7,308	13	46
3 months	2,268	8	54	2,828	5	51
4 months	1,299	5	59	1,227	2	53
5 months	895	3	62	478	1	54
6 months	191	1	63	438	1	55
6–12 months	1,086	4	67	1,406	3	58
1–4 years	1,685	6	73	619	1	59
4–8 years	2,566	9	82	5,193	10	69
8–12 years	1,831	7	89	3,914	7	76
12–16 years	1,503	5	94	3,695	6	82
More than 16 years	1,613	6	100	9,611	18	100
Total	27,944	100	—	54,430	100	—

a. Health-related absences caused by combined effects of background illnesses and medical injuries.

b. Includes durations of absence from household work among female workers.

Note: Percentages are rounded.

losses was attributable to the minority of patients who died: for example, the 18 percent of injured workers who died represented 66 percent of the total wages lost.

As one would expect, retired persons were the largest consumers of health care services, reflecting the fact that the prevalence of chronic degenerative diseases and the consequent need for long-term care increase with age. Patients who suffered from a disability prior to their 1984 hospitalization had the next highest average use of medical care.

Figure 5.1a   Distribution of patients by duration of work absences

Figure 5.1b   Distribution of patients by duration of household absences

Table 5.2 Estimated costs of medical injuries to adults (millions of undiscounted dollars)

Type of loss	Total costs of illness and injury	Costs of injury alone			
		Control-experimental comparison		Physician attribution	
		$	% of total costs	$	% of total costs
Earnings	2,453	420	17	467	19
Household production	3,379	884	26	1,497	44
Subtotal	5,832	1,304	22	1,964	34
Medical care	14,462	—	—	1,805	12
Total	20,294	—	—	3,769	19

Note: — = not estimated.

COSTS ATTRIBUTABLE TO MEDICAL INJURY

The figures just presented depict the aggregate losses experienced by injured patients as a consequence of *both* their medical injury and their original illness. The next step in our analysis was to estimate the financial costs attributable to the injury alone. We found that iatrogenic injury was responsible for only a small proportion of the total costs, but that the distributional pattern was quite similar in the two sources of loss.

We employed the two methodologies described earlier for purposes of disentangling the cost of injuries from the cost of illness in the case of adult patients. Table 5.2 presents estimates derived via both methods. As the table shows, approximately one-fifth of the total costs stemmed from iatrogenic injury, but the estimates for specific categories of loss varied with the method used.

For lost earnings, probably the most significant component of any new compensation plan, the two methods present reasonably close (and thus mutually reinforcing) estimates in the range of $450 million, or roughly one-fifth the aggregate cost of illness and injury combined. The most unstable estimates relate to the effects of medical injury on household production: this is the factor that was most difficult for our physicians to isolate on the basis of only the written records available to them (particularly since there is no litmus test regarding performance of household work that corresponds to the simple fact of whether or not a person is employed). The fact that the physician attribution estimate ($1.5 billion) was nearly double the figure ($884 million) generated by our between-group comparisons reflects the operating presumption we used in cases of uncertain attribution, namely, that the decision should favor injury rather than underlying illness as the true cause of the loss. (And because we used only the physician attribution results as the basis for our calculation of potentially compensable losses under a no-fault plan, the costs assumed for the household production factor in that plan are likely to be overestimated.) Finally, potentially compensable medical costs, estimated through physician attribution alone, amounted to $1.8 billion, or about 12 percent of total medical costs from the disease episode as a whole.

DISTRIBUTION OF IATROGENIC INJURY LOSSES

As is apparent from Figure 5.2 (based on the physician attribution method), iatrogenic injury losses exhibit the same distributional pattern depicted earlier for aggregate losses: most injured patients suffer very small losses, while a handful suffer huge ones. With respect to medical expenditures, for example, the lifetime cost of the medical care caused by adverse events was less than $4,000 for more than half the patients who were injured. Even more striking, lost wages and lost household production (which is much less likely to be covered by insurance) total less than $4,000 for more than 85 percent of injured patients. This distribution tracks the pattern noted earlier, that within less than six months nearly two-thirds of injured living workers had returned to employment and 45 percent of injured homemakers had resumed their household duties. (The difference in these percentages is accounted for by the fact that a disproportionate number of elderly women died as a result of adverse events in their treatment.) At the other pole, though, about 3 percent of injured patients incurred more than $100,000 each in lifetime medical treatment expenditures, and approximately the same proportion incurred that much in lost wages or household production.

Another interesting disparity occurs between victims of negligent and non-negligent injuries. We saw in Chapter 3 that whereas neg-

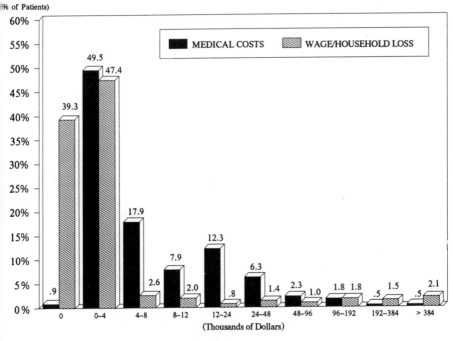

% of Patients)

Figure 5.2 Distribution of adult patients by lifetime costs of medical care plus losses of wages and household production caused by medical injuries

ligent injuries comprised roughly one-quarter of total medical injuries, they made up from 40 to 50 percent of the severe to fatal injuries. Unsurprisingly, then, the economic losses suffered by the negligently injured adults were sharply higher as well: 60 percent greater wage losses per case and 240 percent greater household production losses. On the other hand, the average medical expenses among the negligently injured were sharply lower, an ironic result of the fact that negligence inflicted a disproportionate share of *fatal* injuries, the cases without long-term medical costs.

COMPENSABLE ADULT LOSSES UNDER NO-FAULT
INSURANCE
The preceding section depicted the size and distribution of the social costs attributable to medical injury, including not only the costs borne

by individual victims and their families but also those distributed to the broader community through a variety of insurance arrangements. Taken together with the nonfinancial consequences of medical injury—pain and suffering, loss of enjoyment of life, and loss of companionship and support for the families of deceased or disabled victims—these estimated economic costs give some indication of why it might be worthwhile for the health care system to invest significant resources in procedures and equipment that will reduce the risks of medical injury. But in designing a no-fault compensation plan for individual patient-victims, not all of the social costs need be accounted for. The larger community already bears a significant share of this burden, through either health insurance for medical expenditures or tax revenues lost from disabled or deceased workers. In this section we present more precise estimates of the costs of compensable benefits that would be payable under a no-fault plan with the design features explained earlier in this chapter.

Table 5.3 summarizes the cost adjustments and payments for adult victims of medical injuries. All these figures are based on case-by-case physician attributions, which simulated the procedures that would be followed by any no-fault program for appraising individual claims. The major adjustment to the earlier social cost estimates was the offset for amounts received from various sources of direct insurance. Additional adjustments were made for income taxes otherwise payable on lost earnings, an allowance for the personal consumption of decedents from their earnings or household production, and a six-month deductible period running from the date of admission to the hospital. (Later we will present the additional program expenditures that would result if the deductible were reduced from six months to zero.)

With respect to medical care estimates, for example, projected total costs are reduced tenfold, from $1.8 billion to $180 million. By far the largest adjustment is the offset for health insurance benefits, which takes projected costs all the way down to $240 million; the six-month deductible accounts for another $34 million. With respect to lost earnings, total wage losses of $467 million attributable to medical injury are reduced to $256 million when personal consumption and income taxes from those earnings are taken into account. Because long-term disability insurance is much less wide-

Table 5.3 Compensable costs of adverse events: injured adults ($million)[a]

Type of loss or cost	$million
Gross wage losses	2,453
Losses attributable to adverse events	467
Less: Income taxes	−103
Consumption payments	−108
Compensation payments	−55
Deductible period losses (6 months)	−18
Plus: Net loss of fringe benefits	34
Compensable Wage Loss	217
(Present value)	(208)
Gross costs of medical care	14,462
Costs attributable to adverse events	1,805
Less: Compensation from health insurance	−1,565
Deductible period costs (6 months)	−61
Compensable costs of care	179
(Present value)	(135)
Gross losses of household production	3,379
Losses attributed to adverse events	1,497
Less: Consumption deductions	−895
Deductible period losses (6 months)	−34
Compensable loss of household production	568
(Present value)	(441)
Total compensable costs	964
(Present value)	(784)

a. All values are for the base year 1984, except "present values," which are in 1989 dollars.

Note: $N = 703$; population = 90,882.

spread than health care insurance, the offset for this factor reduces compensable wage loss by only 20 percent ($55 million). The six-month waiting period accounts for a mere $18 million deduction, only half the $34 million that is added by our assumption that lost fringe benefits should be included in compensable earnings.

Finally, the total cost figure for lost household production, $1.5 billion, goes all the way down to $600 million simply by allowing for the victim's personal consumption, since a high proportion of this category of loss stemmed from the large number of medical fatalities in the homemaker-patient category. Another $34 million is

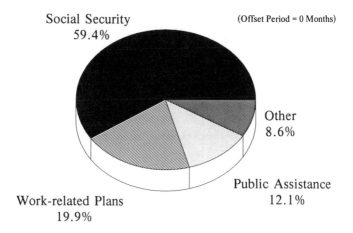

Social Security
59.4%

(Offset Period = 0 Months)

Other
8.6%

Public Assistance
12.1%

Work-related Plans
19.9%

Figure 5.3 Compensation to workers for disability or death, by source

deductible for the six-month factor, but none for insurance payments, which are unavailable for this category of loss. As we said earlier, the net undiscounted loss of $568 million is probably somewhat inflated because making physician attributions of this factor from written records is so difficult.

LOSS INSURANCE BENEFITS
Our data about loss insurance benefits are useful not just for estimating the compensable losses under what we assume would be second-payor no-fault insurance, but also for what they reveal about the availability of such coverage for the victims of medical (and presumably other types of) accidents (Figure 5.3).

For example, with respect to earnings losses, work-related sick leave payments from employers and benefits from New York's Temporary Disability Insurance Plan were an important source of income replacement, totaling more than $90 million, or 20 percent of such benefits for injured patients. The vast bulk of this amount is not reflected in Table 5.3, however, because the benefits were paid during and for the six-month deductible period (and also because disability payments were deducted only for persons who actually suffered losses in take-home earnings). By contrast, the federal social security system provided the majority of earnings replacement for longer-

term disabilities, which would be the principal focus of our hypothetical no-fault plan. While public and private disability insurance
replaced only about one-sixth of the net lost wages from long-term
iatrogenic injuries or fatalities, this aggregate share disguises the
actual distribution of the uncompensated losses. For example, of all
victims with wage losses after six months, approximately one-quarter
were fully reimbursed (or better) for their losses, while the other
three-quarters had uncompensated losses estimated to average
$70,000 apiece. And it appears that among patients who sued there
were sharply higher levels of economic loss, as well as a much lower
ratio of compensation for such losses, than among patients who did
not sue. This helps explain our findings in Chapter 4 that more
malpractice suits are brought by patients without rather than with a
negligent medical injury.

THE DEDUCTIBLE PERIOD

The design of the no-fault program for which we were estimating
compensable costs included a deductible period running from the
date the patient was first admitted to the hospital. This rule was
intended to serve two purposes: to reduce the administrative difficulty of trying to disentangle losses attributable to injury rather than
illness in the early treatment and recuperation period; and to target
the program's benefit dollars at the people with the most serious
losses. (Their losses are greater because earnings are lost over a longer
period and because long-term disability insurance is much less prev-
alent than short-term sick-leave pay.) The other side of the coin is
that, unlike many no-fault workers' compensation systems, the program we envisaged placed no upper limit on the duration and
amount of such medical accident compensation.

In initial estimates for our report to New York State, we used six
months as the relevant time frame because that period dovetailed
with the transition from the state's temporary disability program to
federal social security disability insurance. There is, of course, no
immutable logic in choosing six months as the waiting period for
no-fault medical injury benefits, and objections have been made that
in certain cases a waiting period this long would cause great hard-
ship. So we reexamined our data to estimate what additional financial costs would ensue from reducing that deductible month by

Table 5.4 Compensable costs and numbers of beneficiaries for different offset periods: injured adults

Offset period (months)	Wage loss benefits		Medical care payments		Household benefits		Total (excludes fringe	
	Payments ($million)	Payees (000s)	Payments ($million)	Payees (000s)	Payments ($million)	Payees (000s)	Payments ($million)	Paye (000
0	201	10.6	240	60.5	602	37.3	1,043	76.
1	196	4.6	214	43.3	588	11.5	998	47.
2	192	3.2	199	38.9	581	6.8	972	42.
3	189	2.9	192	37.2	578	5.6	959	40.
4	187	2.7	187	36.4	575	5.0	949	39.
5	185	2.5	182	35.9	573	4.2	940	39.
6	183	2.5	179	35.1	568	4.0	930	38.

Note: Overlaps among categories have been eliminated.

month. The results of that exercise for all adult victims' losses are described in Table 5.4 and Figure 5.4. It is evident that in aggregate terms the benefit cost savings from this deductible are comparatively modest: in undiscounted dollars, this factor reduces total cost by approximately 10 percent (from $1.043 billion to $930 million). On the other hand, the number of cases in which benefits would be payable (therefore in which administrative decisions would have to be made about whether and to what extent medical injury occurred) doubled overall, quadrupled for wage loss benefits, and went up tenfold for household production. The explanation for this pattern lies in the data we presented earlier about the extremely skewed distribution of disability duration among patient-victims.

These figures indicate the nature of the trade-off that must be made in designing a sensible no-fault medical insurance plan. While we are convinced that some deductible period is required to exclude the largest number of the most difficult-to-call cases, Table 5.4 shows that a two-month deductible period secures the bulk of this administrative gain, particularly with respect to the more troublesome determinations of wage loss and household production benefits. This significant extension in program coverage, from six months back to

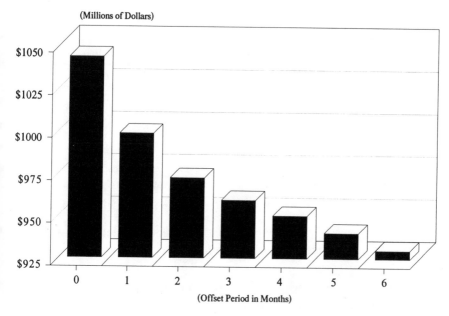

Figure 5.4   Compensable costs by offset durations

two months, can be purchased at the modest additional expense of $42 million in benefit payments.

CHILDREN'S LOSSES

Our results for children are presented separately because the number of injured children in our patient sample was rather small, and so our projections of lifetime costs for children were less precise. From our sample we estimate that 416 children hospitalized in New York in 1984 suffered compensable episodes of disability attributable to medical injuries. The projected social costs from these disability episodes totaled $581 million in medical expenditures and $123 million in future lost wages. Medical care insurance would reduce the individual children's compensable medical cost to $82 million. Because of the small size of our sample and the long period over which such losses had to be forecast, we did not adjust wage loss figures for fringe benefits, taxes, personal consumption, or disability insurance benefits, as we had for adult earners. The net effect of these omissions

Table 5.5 Present values of net compensable costs of adverse events ($million)[a]

	Workers	Adult nonworkers	Children	Total
Wages	208	—	68	276
Medical care	44	91	26	161
Lost household production	170	271	—	441
Total	422	362	94	878

a. Present values for base year 1984, expressed in 1989 dollars.

was that our $123 million figure somewhat overstates the likely compensable wage losses of children.

TOTAL DISCOUNTED COMPENSABLE COSTS
OF NO-FAULT INSURANCE
The last step in our calculation was to discount the projected lifetime compensable costs of injury to a present value, using the 2.75 percent real interest rate factor referred to earlier. Table 5.5 incorporates the compensable cost totals for each of our patient categories and each of the covered types of loss (assuming a six-month deductible period). The bottom-line result is that benefit costs in 1989 dollars for all compensable losses suffered by New York patients hospitalized in 1984 would have totaled $878 million: the cost would be $923 million with a two-month deductible. Of this total, roughly half ($451 million of the $878 million) would constitute payments to negligently injured patients, who tended to suffer severe long-term or fatal medical injuries.

Implications

How should we assess the significance of this approximately $900 million cost figure? From an immediate "affordability" point of view, the natural comparison is with the costs of existing malpractice insurance, which we estimate at more than $1 billion in 1988 for all doctors and hospitals in New York.[22] A number of important issues must be addressed, though, before any policy implications can fairly be drawn from direct comparison of these two figures.

The first of these issues are methodological. With respect to definition, calculation, and projection of the financial consequences of disability, we built on techniques developed for similar surveys of the victims of aviation, motor vehicle, occupational, and product accidents. However, we faced the additional difficulty of disentangling the disabling consequences of iatrogenic injuries from those produced by the underlying illness itself (a problem analogous to the challenge described in Chapter 3 of determining whether a medical injury had occurred in the first place).

Our experience was that given an identifiable patient injury in the medical records, we could readily attribute subsequent spells of disability to either the injury or the initial illness. For this purpose we used both the original hospital record and the patient's report in the survey interview about what had transpired since hospitalization. Particularly with respect to time lost from work, few cases were difficult to categorize, and there was a high level of agreement among reviewers. We assumed that the entire disability was compensable unless the reviewer was confident that only a portion of the disabling effect was caused by the medical injury. Consequently, our cost estimates based on the physician attribution method are likely to err on the high side.

A totally different methodology—the experimental–control group comparison—provided important corroboration for the physician-attribution results. The between-group analysis compared the post-hospitalization experience of two matched groups of patients, one with and the other without iatrogenic injury, to identify the aggregate results of adverse medical events without any need for individualized attribution.

With respect to lost wages, the between-group comparison estimate—$420 million—was within 10 percent of the $467 million figure arrived at by the markedly different attribution technique. On the other hand, there was a wide disparity between the household production costs derived from the between-group comparison ($884 million) and those derived from physician attribution ($1.497 billion). The much higher second figure testifies to the difficulty of determining from a paper record the precise source of someone's inability to do household work, especially years after an initial illness and hospitalization, and reflects our criterion that in uncertain situations, losses would be attributed to injury rather than to underlying illness. Our projection of the lost household production component of a patient compensation scheme is likely, therefore, to be considerably inflated.

Even if our estimates of the costs of those factors we did address are reasonably accurate, we emphasize that our estimates do not include all the important components of a no-fault compensation program. For example, substantial additional allowance must be made for the cost of administration. Under the existing medical malpractice system approximately 55 cents of the claims dollar is spent on legal administration rather than on direct payments to victims.[23]

We did not attempt to estimate the likely administrative costs of no-fault patient compensation. But workers' compensation, the best-known example of the no-fault model, spends roughly only 20 cents of the claims dollar on administration.[24] A principal source of this cost saving by comparison to malpractice is the absence of litigation over the defendant's fault: reliance is placed on a less-formal administrative determination of what caused the victim's injury. In conducting the hospital records review, we found that the proportion of close calls in judgments about medical causation was roughly one-quarter of that proportion in judgments about provider negligence. We believe, though, that the workers' compensation experience is likely to suggest a floor rather than a ceiling for the additional cost of patient compensation. Thus, we would add another 30 to 35 percent to the $900 million benefit cost figure provided earlier.

Even more difficult questions of policy are posed by the judgments we made about which benefit categories should be compensated in a no-fault scheme. One of us has set forth elsewhere the pros and cons of these issues.[25] Here we shall simply make some brief observations about the basis and implications of our judgments.

Our most notable omitted category is "pain and suffering," the legal rubric for the many forms of nonpecuniary loss of enjoyment of life experienced by accident victims. As we noted at the outset of this chapter, this category of damages now accounts for roughly 50 percent of the amount of tort awards, in medical malpractice as well as in other fields, such as product litigation. Scholars in the personal injury field now believe that this type of loss is a dubious candidate for compensation by any type of insurance. If any funds at all are to be expended for this purpose, they argue, the preferred method is a reasonably modest, easily administered schedule of benefit payments for the permanently disabled, as exists now under a number of workers' compensation programs.[26] Although we have made no allowance for this benefit category, our interviews included questions about present levels of physical impairment. We are currently embarked on an effort to determine the potential costs of a scheduled financial benefit for impairment of normal enjoyment of life. When completed, our data will give policymakers a more informed basis upon which to decide whether the health care system should provide this kind of redress to the victims of iatrogenic injuries.

Even with respect to pecuniary losses, we made important assumptions about certain constraints on the benefits payable. Here we reiterate the rationale for two of these assumptions.

One such assumption, that there should be a waiting period before no-fault benefits are payable, was important more for administrative than for financial reasons. Establishing such a time frame from the date of hospital admission would reduce the problem of disentangling the harmful consequences of the original illness from those attributable to the iatrogenic injury itself, a problem that is most acute in the early stages of disability. In addition, a six-month "deductible" would serve to channel scarce funds to victims who suffer the largest losses and are least likely to be covered by other sources of coverage, such as sick pay for time lost from work.

As Table 5.4 demonstrated, our original six-month selection excluded only about 10 percent of potentially compensable losses but cut in half the number of potential claimants posing potentially troublesome administrative decisions. However, further reducing the deductible period to two months and thereby covering all but modest short-term losses causes benefit expenditures to rise by only 5 percent, and the lion's share of difficult-to-call cases of short-term losses of wages and household production is still screened out.

From the point of view of the financial affordability of no-fault medical accident compensation, our most important assumption was that such a program should function as a secondary payor to direct health care insurance (which covers 80 percent of medical costs) and disability insurance (which covers 20 percent of lost wages). In our view that arrangement is most sensible because loss insurance coverage does not require the expense and delay of making the inevitably contestable judgments about medical causation. Moreover, assigning a backstop role to medical no-fault accords with the emerging consensus in medical malpractice litigation, which has led many states (including New York) to adopt rules that offset against potential tort awards any amounts payable for victims' losses from other forms of insurance.

Our tables indicate that this factor is a major source of savings in the cost estimates for no-fault, because health care insurance covers roughly 80 percent of medical expenses and disability insurance roughly 20 percent of long-term loss of earnings. We note, however, that one deduction reflected in our calculation—payments under Medicare and Medicaid—may well be unavailable under present federal regulations.[27] If the federal government were not prepared to waive its present reimbursement claims for payments made to victims enjoying rights under a no-fault compensation scheme, our cost estimates would rise by another $250 million.

With such an addition for Medicare and Medicaid, a comparable one for administrative costs, and allowance for even a modest schedule of pain-and-suffering benefits, the $878 million figure stated earlier could easily increase to around $1.5 billion, an amount that is clearly larger than the cost of present-day malpractice liability (although this is so only if one counts liability premiums alone and ignores the costs of unnecessary defensive medicine that the tort system may now induce). However, these comparative figures must be considered with two important qualifications in mind.

First, although some additional program funds could be included for pain and suffering, these funds would be offset by a considerably smaller, more realistic estimate of benefits that would probably be payable for lost household production. (Recall that in outlining a no-fault scheme that excluded pain and suffering, we generously valued those benefits at full market earnings for any losses of this type that were even arguably iatrogenic, losses that were then projected for the full life expectancy of the injured patient.)

Second, our estimate of the cost of no-fault patient compensation is based on systematic identification of *all* patient injuries and losses attributable to medical intervention and thus potentially covered by such a program. Although some dubious claims would probably be made and paid at the margin of any such entitlement program, a considerable proportion of valid claims would never be brought, because many patients would be unable to identify earlier medical treatment as the source of their disability. By contrast, the current insurance costs for malpractice litigation are a function of actual claims made and paid, in a setting in which a huge litigation gap now exists.

Indeed, our breakdown of economic losses between those suffered as a result of negligent as opposed to non-negligent injuries underscores the compensation deficiencies of the existing malpractice system, even on its own terms. The corrective justice roots of fault-based tort liability presume that the victims of negligent harm have a moral claim to legal redress. But although negligently injured patients suffer a disproportionate share of the financial losses inflicted on our patient group, the law's insistence that medical accident victims identify and demonstrate their providers' fault has meant that merely a tiny fraction of "deserving" victims ever realize on the tort rights to which they are supposedly entitled. That pattern is not only unwarranted in principle; it also is probably unstable in practice. Doctors' experience in the 1970s and the 1980s provides no assurance that present levels of malpractice litigation and premiums are destined to endure.

At a minimum, this chapter has demonstrated that a reasonably comprehensive patient compensation scheme—which would fully reimburse all actual longer-term financial losses that patients suffer as a result of iatrogenic injury—would be a small and readily affordable item in the budget of the health care system that generates these injuries (and, in New York, thereby necessitates nearly $2 billion in additional health care expenditures to treat and care for the injured patients). Affordability, of course, is only one concern in the debate about alternatives to malpractice litigation. Quality of care is an even more vital aspect of the debate. Whether existing fault-based liability or a no-fault or strict liability alternative can generate effective incentives for safer medical treatment is the subject of another major component of our study, described in the next chapter.

Malpractice Litigation and Injury Prevention

Objectives

In the previous chapter we concluded that for approximately the same amount of money now spent on medical malpractice liability we could extend insurance protection for important financial needs to far more medical accident victims than now collect any money through tort. In that respect, our research provides explicit confirmation of the general impression that tort is an erratic and uneconomic mode of compensation. Unsurprisingly, then, defenders of the malpractice regime rely for justification principally on the contribution of litigation to medical injury prevention.

Even though the Harvard Medical Practice Study documented the broader shortcomings of malpractice law as a source of compensation, the fact is that one can observe money being delivered through litigation into the hands of some patients suffering from serious physical injury. By contrast, it is possibly only by inference, not by observation, to make the deterrence connection between the actions of the legal system—holding doctors liable for malpractice in the courtroom—and the reactions of the health care system—improving the quality of medical practice in the operating room. That is why we invested a great deal of time and effort in trying to quantify the preventive impact of malpractice law. We surveyed a broad sample of New York physicians on their experience with and perception of tort litigation; we then analyzed whether variations in the intensity of that litigation experience across the state appeared to produce a detectable impact on the incidence of provider negligence and patient injury in our statewide hospital sample.

It is natural to assume that the tort system has some deterrent impact. What malpractice litigation sets out to do is to identify those providers who have engaged in careless treatment and then require doctors and others found at fault to pay for the consequent damages inflicted on their patients. The prospect that negligent behavior will be penalized in this fashion should give all providers a real incentive to be careful in their medical practice. In that regard tort law rests on the same commonsense notions of deterrence that influence human behavior in fields ranging from child rearing to criminal justice to defense policy.

However, a distinctive characteristic of the tort system is that its penalties are meted out if and only if one person's lack of care actually inflicts injury on someone else. Moreover, the size of the legal penalty is the measure of monetary damages needed to provide full redress for the harm inflicted on the victim. Critics of the tort regime regularly object, then, that there is only a fortuitous connection between the gravity of the actor's fault and the severity of the victim's injury.

Sophisticated economic analysis has shown that, if it operates in line with its ideal assumptions, tort law can contribute to achievement of the optimal level of care—defined as avoidance of the risk of injuries that are costlier than the precautions needed to prevent them.[1] Malpractice law, in effect, establishes a price for the harmful result to a patient injured in a medical accident, and then assesses this price against those providers who fail to undertake the precautions—such as diagnostic tests—that, despite their immediate costs, are still a worthwhile investment in avoiding the risk of the severe injury that occurred.

The flip side of the current fault-based tort law is that if it is not reasonable (that is, not cost effective) for an actor to adopt a particular precaution, then the injury losses are to be borne by the victims themselves. However, such denial of legal liability in the absence of fault does not necessarily follow from imposition of liability in the presence of fault. As we shall explain in the next chapter, it is possible to design a strict liability regime for medical injuries, modeled on present-day workers' compensation for occupational injuries, that would impose on the health care provider involved the costs of all injuries, including those injuries not now avoidable through reasonable measures. In principle, such additional legal responsibility under a no-fault program would not detract from providers' current financial incentive to undertake reasonable measures to prevent injuries that can now be avoided; moreover, it would also serve to compensate—and perhaps eventually to reduce—those injuries that cannot now be prevented.[2]

The assumption of either the current fault-based system or the alternative model of strict liability is that imposing the legal costs of at least negligent injuries on the responsible party serves as an effective incentive for accident prevention. Yet a number of practical obstacles impede the tort system's performance of this preventive role, particularly in the medical field.

A special problem, documented in Chapter 4, is the low probability that any one negligent injury, even a severe or fatal injury, will produce a tort claim, let alone a tort payment. To the extent that injured victims systematically underutilize their tort rights, there is a corresponding reduction in actors' incentives to adopt socially optimal precautions against such injuries.

Arguably this is not as serious a problem for medical malpractice as it might be for products liability, for example, because of the actors' differing situations in these respective areas. Doctors have a special altruistic concern for the well-being of their patients. Even in self-interested terms, doctors do not face the same kinds of monetary incentives that manufacturers do to economize on safety. Many of the tests and procedures that doctors may undertake to avoid patient injuries and tort suits (such as doing a Caesarean rather than a normal delivery) are in fact financially advantageous to the doctor; moreover, they impose little or no additional cost on (and thence price resistance from) the patient who is insured for such health care services.

Present malpractice law tacitly acknowledges the special features of the medical context by deliberately abstaining from independent jury evaluation of the reasonableness of the customary standards of treatment developed within the medical profession. Such legal restraint is in marked contrast to the law's readiness to scrutinize and second-guess the practices of prescription drug manufacturers, for example. Malpractice litigation contents itself with enforcing rather than defining the appropriate standard of physician care, by penalizing doctors who deviate from the profession's customary standards—standards that are likely to be more rather than less safety conscious than would seem optimal.[3]

At the same time, sharp debate flourishes among legal scholars about the efficacy of tort law in performing even that more modest deterrence role.[4] Some question whether the threat of tort sanctions influences doctors in their daily practice, a setting in which most negligence consists in a failure to be conscious of and attentive to the dangers in the patient's condition or the doctor's mode of treatment, rather than in a deliberately planned decision to run an unreasonable risk with the patient's safety. Others note that however sizable the tort penalty may be if it is indeed inflicted, the prospect that such a penalty will ever be levied is remote. They argue, then, that the deterrent force of tort litigation is weaker than that of milder disciplinary measures which can be routinely and expeditiously applied.

The most common and fundamental criticism of tort law as a mode of prevention is that any possible deterrent force of the tort award has been removed because the award is no longer paid by the individual doctor who may have been careless, but instead by a malpractice insurance carrier that collects premiums from all such doctors, careful and careless alike. This critique is not directed against liability insurance itself: that institution serves to protect the doctor from possibly crushing damages as a result of a momentary inadvertent mishap and also guarantees that the patient who has been hurt will find a source of funds to pay the damage verdict won in the courtroom. But the presence of this insurance buffer between the doctor and the tort sanction has persuaded many that we should place little independent weight on the supposed deterrent value of malpractice litigation as an instrument for enhancing the quality of medical care.

To be sure, insurance and prevention are not inevitably incompatible. It is possible to devise a system for pricing the insurance policy that would incorporate premium surcharges and rebates based on the actual claims experience of individual insureds and thus build into the liability insurance the deterrent threat that has apparently been removed from the tort process. Although such an experience-rating program is widespread in fields such as workers' compensation, in which larger firms face hundreds, even thousands, of employee compensation claims every year, it has not found much favor with the carriers that insure individual doctors against malpractice suits, which are still only an occasional event in the doctors' lives. It simply has not proved feasible to develop a formula that is an actuarially credible measure of the relative risk posed by individual doctors and that also generates premium adjustments large enough to serve as a meaningful financial incentive for enough doctors to make a tangible impact on the incidence of patient injuries.[5]

Nevertheless, the attention paid to liability insurance with or without experience rating obscures the fact that an insurance policy is by no means a complete buffer between the doctor and the tort process. Although the carrier will pay any tort awards or settlements (as well as the costs of defending against these legal outcomes), the individual doctor still suffers serious negative consequences as a result of being involved in such litigation. These consequences include financial losses from practice time and revenues that are foregone while the doctor is consulting with lawyers, reviewing and producing records, undergoing depositions, and attending the trial. Even more disquieting may be the psychological stress that results when a doctor is the target of a lawsuit brought by his own patient, when he sees the quality of his care and competence attacked in open court, and perhaps has his professional reputation stigmatized by an adverse jury verdict (which itself may cause future loss of patients and referrals). These immediate and entirely uninsured consequences of being sued and found liable probably dwarf any statistically valid increase in the doctor's future malpractice premiums from experience rating.[6]

Of course, reliance by malpractice law on these kinds of personal, uninsured costs of litigation removes any correspondence between the award paid to the patient and the penalty paid by the doctor— a correspondence that was assumed in an optimally functioning system of tort incentives. More important, the bulk of these costs of litigation are inflicted on doctors as a result of merely being sued rather than as a result of ultimately being found liable. Recall from Chapter 4, however, the finding that in terms of absolute numbers more claims are filed against careful than against careless doctors. To reiterate the analogy from that chapter, one cannot assume that a legal regime that gives out more traffic tickets to drivers going through an intersection on the green than on the red light will serve as an effective deterrent against drivers going through on the red.

These ambivalent conclusions from armchair speculation about malpractice deterrence underscore the need for serious empirical investigation of this topic. We have not had the benefit of research that documents the ability of malpractice litigation to reduce iatrogenic injury.[7]

The most substantial body of evidence about the preventive impact of the tort system relates to motor vehicle accidents. In the 1970s a number of states adopted no-fault insurance programs that were either added to or partially substituted for tort liability. Subsequent research about whether this change in the compensation regime affected motor vehicle injury rates produced conflicting results.[8] This ambiguous verdict is not surprising, because the most comprehensive and objective data base for such research concerns *fatal* motor vehicle accidents, but no American no-fault scheme affects the right to sue in tort for such fatal accidents. However, the province of Quebec in Canada did fully replace tort by no-fault compensation for all motor vehicle accidents. Research on the preventive effect of the Quebec program has documented an appreciable increase in fatal injuries, though there is still debate about how and why this increase occurred.[9]

Evidence from the motor vehicle context is not, however, decisive for the medical setting. For example, the potential effect of tort liability would seem considerably greater for motor vehicle injuries, since, as compared with medical accidents, a far higher proportion of negligent vehicular accidents gives rise to tort claims and awards. In addition, the shift to no-fault motor vehicle accident compensation took the form of first-party loss insurance, rather than strict liability imposed on owner-drivers (the latter is analogous to workers' compensation liability imposed on employers). To try to test directly the deterrent impact of present-day malpractice litigation (in part to project the consequences of removing any such liability), we undertook a two-part investigation of this phenomenon in New York.

The first part of the deterrence study consisted of detailed surveys of New York physicians. We aimed to elicit from them the effects felt by doctors who became embroiled in malpractice litigation, their personal impression of the risks they faced of being sued and having to bear these negative consequences, and how doctors viewed the force of the tort signal by comparison to other quality assurance programs in the health care system. The second part of the study sought to discover whether doctors' reactions to the threat of tort suits produced an observable reduction in negligent patient injury. Our hospital record review had revealed a pattern of negligent injuries in 1984 across New York State. Our litigation record review had assembled the entire pool of malpractice claims filed and paid in the years before (as well as after) 1984. With these resources we attempted an econometric analysis of whether or not greater intensity of tort litigation against doctors (with other relevant variables controlled for) produced fewer (negligent) patient injuries.

Methods

PHYSICIAN SURVEY

Two distinct but complementary facets were features of the physician survey. One consisted of a written questionnaire mailed to a broad sample of New York physicians to obtain their responses to a standardized set of questions. The other facet consisted of in-depth personal interviews of selected physicians to explore in greater detail the issues that lay behind the written inquiries.

The physician sample for the mail survey was drawn from the American Medical Association's master file of doctors actively practicing in New York State in 1984. Since we wanted at least 800 participants and we anticipated a response rate of approximately 40 percent, we drew an initial sample of 2,103 physicians.

This representative sample was stratified along three dimensions —specialty, location, and claims history. With respect to specialty, the doctors were distributed among low-risk (internal medicine and associated specialties), medium-risk (general surgery and associated specialties), and high-risk (orthopedic surgeons, neurosurgeons, and obstetricians). With respect to location, the relevant areas of practice were the Long Island counties; New York, Ulster, Orange, and Westchester counties; Bronx, Kings, Queens, Richmond, Rockland, and Sullivan counties; and all the upstate counties. With respect to claims history, we distinguished between doctors who had and those who had not had a claim filed against them since 1975.

Of the 2,103 physicians in our initial sample pool, we were able to locate and mail the survey to 1,823. We received completed questionnaires from 739 physicians, for a 41 percent response rate. The respondents were somewhat more likely than nonrespondents to be older (51 versus 48 years), male (92 versus 86 percent), upstate (32 versus 21 percent), board certified (65 versus 45 percent), and graduates of U.S. medical schools (73 versus 41 percent). Most important, of those for whom we could make a positive comparison with our claims file, 55 percent of our respondents versus 43 percent of our nonrespondents had been the target of at least one malpractice suit since 1975. We corrected for the pattern of nonresponse by adjusting the initial sampling weights accordingly.

Our survey document asked questions about numerous topics that had figured in comparable surveys done in the past. We pretested the survey instrument with a small sample of respondents in order to work out difficulties that physicians might experience in answering specific items.

We sought four major types of information. The first was an estimate of the risk of suit faced by doctors. That risk was specified in different ways: first, the risk of suit per 100 physicians in both the region and the specialty; second, the risk of suit in a particular case, given either a medical injury or a negligent medical injury. These estimates were then compared to the true risks of suit we had calculated from the entire claims base we had assembled in the state and from our matching of claims filed against (negligent) injuries in our patient sample.

The second area of inquiry concerned the financial costs to a doctor resulting from being the target of a malpractice suit. We broke these costs down into days lost from practice in order to defend the suit, out-of-pocket expenses of the doctor for hiring a personal attorney (in addition to the lawyer supplied by the insurer or the hospital in the case), and any direct payments made by a doctor to the patient without recourse to the doctor's liability insurer.

Next we asked our doctors about changes in their pattern of practice over the last ten years. In particular, we wanted to know whether the physician was prone to order more tests and procedures; to take more time explaining to patients the risks of treatment; to spend more time on paperwork, including maintenance of a more detailed patient record; and to see fewer patients and perform fewer clinical procedures. Our aim was to see whether any change in practice behavior was associated with variations in either the perceived risk or the actual experience of being sued.

Finally, we asked our doctors to rate malpractice litigation as an influence for maintaining or enhancing the quality of medical practice, as compared to a variety of other institutional forces: peer relations; morbidity/mortality conferences and tumor boards; medical journals; continuing medical education; the professional review organization (PRO); and clinical care rules, guidelines, or standard operating procedures developed by the departments in the hospital. Each of these potential sources was ranked on a 0-to-5 scale of degrees of influence.

The in-depth personal interviews were designed to complement the mailed questionnaire by adding a qualitative (though not necessarily representative) perspective to the quantitative findings from the broad-based survey. Given a target of approximately 50 interviews, we drew a sample of 102 physicians from the doctors practicing in our hospitals in 1984. The specialties we focused on were obstetrics (high-risk), general surgery (medium-risk), and internal medicine (low-risk). We located 93 of the 102 doctors and were able to interview 47 of them (for a response rate of 51 percent). We pretested the structured interview instrument before proceeding to our main sample.

The approximately 90-minute session in the doctors' offices explored the interviewees' beliefs about why they had been sued (for those who had been), their perception of the impact of litigation on practice, and their attitudes toward other quality assurance programs. Here our objective was to cast further light on why the broad representative sample responded as it did to the corresponding items in the mailed survey. We then presented to our interviewees a series of carefully prepared case examples of patient disability, with varying indicia of adverse events and negligent adverse events in the treatment described. Our objective here was to discern the attitudes of doctors themselves to these crucial questions of causation and negligence in the practice of medicine.

ECONOMETRIC ANALYSIS

The results of our two-part physician survey—which was considerably more ambitious and detailed than similar efforts that had preceded us—depicted the way physicians perceived and reacted to malpractice litigation. The final component of the study, an econometric analysis of our data, undertook to find out what effect actual variations in malpractice litigation might have had on patient injuries. Our aim was to determine whether doctors' reactions to the threat or the reality of litigation had in turn produced observably safer medical care.

We had reservations from the outset about whether analysis of the available data could generate scientifically conclusive results. Ideally, study of the impact of the tort system would compare a jurisdiction that was subject to tort law with another that was not in order to determine what net difference this variable made in physician practice and patient injury. That was the approach followed in the motor vehicle studies referred to earlier, which compared fatality rates in jurisdictions in which or at times when tort law governed with the rates in other jurisdictions in which or at other times when no-fault prevailed (in whole or in part). We did not have the luxury of such a clear-cut legal contrast for medical injuries, because all our data came from New York, a single state formally governed by the same malpractice rules. We had, however, collected for the first time a comprehensive data base of both medical injury rates and claims rates. These data disclosed differences in the likelihood that a patient would sue a doctor in one part of the state or another. Following the lead of studies on the impact of workers' compensation programs or occupational safety and health regulations on workplace injuries, we set out to analyze what impact, if any, was discernible on (negligent) medical injuries from one hospital to another as a result of variations in the intensity of use of the formally identical malpractice regime across New York State. By analogy, on highways where there is more vigorous police enforcement of the same speeding or drunk driving statutes, one might seek to find fewer motor vehicle accidents and injuries.

Unlike the workplace injury studies, however, which could analyze data about a large number of employers across the nation, we had only the medical injury data laboriously gathered from 51 hospitals in a single state. Trying to tease out a connection between medical injury and malpractice litigation from such a limited sample posed major methodological challenges, which we addressed through the decisions described below.

Because we were concerned about the completeness of the litigation numbers reported by two of the hospitals in our sample, we eliminated these hospitals from this part of our work. The litigation data base consisted of all the claims opened and closed from 1980 onward against each hospital and against each physician in our sample. To define the malpractice threat for purposes of our analysis, we used claims opened in 1983, because this was the year just prior to our 1984 sample of hospital admissions and thus most likely to have influenced the mode of treatment and patient injury rates in 1984. We summed all claims against both hospitals and individual physicians on the hospital staffs in order to arrive at an overall measure of the malpractice threat occurring in different hospitals.[10]

On the other side of the statistical coin were the (negligent) medical injuries. These data came from our review (described in Chapter 3) of more than 30,000 hospital records. Some of the injuries and negligence depicted in the hospital charts occurred prior to the index admissions that were being sampled—for example, in a physician's office or at another hospital. Of the 1,278 adverse events that we identified in the study (306 of which were negligent), 922 such events (209 negligent) could be specifically linked to treatment in one of the 49 hospitals in our sample. However, in 3 small hospitals we had found no adverse events, and thus the cases for these hospitals were not included in the sample used for the deterrence analysis. That left us with 27,574 patient admissions, in 843 of which the patient suffered a medical injury, of which 189 injuries were due to provider negligence.

We further refined the injury rate variable in our analysis by estimating two regressions in which the dependent variables were, respectively, the likelihood of a negligent injury per medical injury, and the likelihood of a medical injury per hospital admission. The product of these two variables is the rate of negligent injury per admission. However, we chose to break out the "negligent injury per medical injury" variable because this allowed us some control for unmeasured differences in the case mix across hospitals. Sicker patients are candidates for more complex, riskier forms of treatment and are less able to recover quickly from any given treatment insult than patients who are less sick. By expressing the rate of negligent injury per medical injury rather than simply per admission, we removed a variation in injury rates that is more properly attributable to the case mix served by a particular hospital rather than to the standard of care practiced there.

Having carefully gathered these two bodies of data, injury rates and litigation rates, we faced a basic problem in trying to link the two together. A principal assumption of the tort system, the one we were seeking to test, is that the higher the number of malpractice claims against providers (in other words, the greater the intensity of tort enforcement), the fewer the number of negligent medical injuries that will befall patients. However, tort litigation operates very differently from the highway traffic or occupational safety analogies used earlier, in which tickets are supposed to be issued and fines imposed whenever the proscribed behavior occurs and is observed. Malpractice claims are supposed to be filed only when the provider's negligence inflicts an injury on the patient. Though many claims are filed when there is no negligent injury, the odds that a claim will be filed are far higher when there is a negligent injury. Viewed after the fact, then, the more negligent injuries that occur in a hospital practice, the *more* tort claims one will observe against the hospital. But the logic of tort deterrence is that, viewed before the fact, the more malpractice claims there are, the *fewer* negligent injuries there should be. This problem of reciprocal causality—endogeneity, to use the technical term—posed the fundamental methodological challenge in our analysis: how could we tease out of our data the causal effect of tort claims on medical injuries when the offsetting impact of injuries on claims would tend to mask the former effect?[11]

Ultimately we decided that the most appropriate measure of the tort threat was the rate of claims per negligent injury.[12] Building the influence of injuries on claims directly into our measure of the claims threat would permit us to isolate the effect that variations in the claims threat had on injuries themselves. This methodological refinement also seemed to present a more apt picture of differing intensity in tort deterrence. By analogy with highway traffic enforcement, for example, suppose we learn that in one hospital (or on one highway) there is 1 tort claim (or 1 traffic ticket) for every 2 negligent injuries (or speeding violations): the law is displaying more teeth here than in another setting in which there is just 1 claim (or ticket) for every 10 injuries (or violations). That ranking holds true even if in the latter setting there is 1 claim (or ticket) for every 500 hospital discharges (or licensed drivers), versus 1 per 1,000 hospital discharges (or licensed drivers) in the former.[13]

Had we simply regressed the proportion of negligent events on claims per negligent event, however, we would have inflated the estimate of the relationship between the tort threat and the injury rate. The reason is that the number of negligent injuries appears both in the numerator of the key dependent variable (negligent adverse events per adverse events) and in the denominator of the explanatory variable of greatest interest (claims per negligent event). Inevitable measurement error in any estimate of the number of adverse events drawn from a sample would induce a spurious negative correlation between these two variables.

A standard econometric technique that is used to address this problem, as well as that of reciprocal causality, is known as instrumental variables.[14] With this technique one uses as the explanatory variable a predicted level of claims per negligent event, rather than actual claims per event. To use this technique it is necessary to isolate one or more variables that predict the likelihood that a claim will be brought but that are not directly related to the occurrence of either a negligent injury or a medical injury.

The instrumental variables we selected for this purpose were the percentage of the population that is urban in the hospital's county and the population density in this county.[15] To guard against the possibility that either urbanization or population density might directly affect the injury rate by influencing the quality of physicians and the level of hospital resources, we controlled for a number of other variables in our equations: the patient's age, race, insurance status, DRG risk group, and location; the hospital's control (public, voluntary, for profit) and teaching status; and the per capita income of the county.[16]

The basic logic of our statistical approach, then, was first to isolate the extent to which differences in population and urban density produced differences in the rates of malpractice claims from one

Table 6.1   Risk of suit perceived by physicians in different specialties[a]

Specialty group	Number of M.D.s responding	Weighted average perceived risk	Standard error	Actual risk, 1986	Ratio perceived/ actual risk
Low-risk	300	12.1	0.9	3.8	3.2
Medium-risk	182	23.4	1.6	10.9	2.1
High-risk	243	34.3	1.7	20.8	1.6
Overall	735	19.5	0.7	6.6	3.0

a. All differences are statistically significant at $p < .001$.

hospital to another. We then examined whether variations in the tort threat accounted for by these instrumental variables (variations that would therefore be free of any effect of negligent injury rates on claims rates) produced an observable difference in the rate of either medical injury (for which we had 843 observations) or negligent injury (189 observations) in our sample of hospitalized patients, controlling for a number of other variables that could also influence quality of provider care and patient injury.

Results

PHYSICIAN SURVEY

An initial important finding from our physician survey was that doctors systematically overestimate the risk that malpractice actions will be brought against them and their colleagues. For example, when asked what was the annual rate of suit per 100 physicians, the average estimate was roughly three times the true rate in New York (see Table 6.1). Doctors did recognize that there were pronounced variations between the higher- and lower-litigation-rate regions (downstate versus upstate) and specialties (surgery and obstetrics versus internal medicine and pediatrics). However, physicians in lower-risk specialties and regions provided even larger overestimates of the chances of being sued than did doctors facing a higher risk.

When the question was posed in another manner—not, what is the annual rate of malpractice claims per 100 doctors? but rather, what is the likelihood of a claim given a patient injury and/or physician negligence?—the resulting overestimate was far greater. On average, New York doctors believe that 45 percent of adverse events and 60 percent of negligent adverse events lead to malpractice claims. Yet even if we ignore the problem of mismatched claims and injuries, the aggregate ratios presented in Chapter 4 indicate that the true ratio of all claims to all negligent injuries was approximately 13 percent, and of claims to injuries, less than 4 percent—an order of magnitude smaller than what doctors believe to be true.

There are two additional intriguing aspects to these physician perceptions. First, doctors assume that there is only a modest increase in the risk of being sued (from 45 to 60 percent) when they are actually negligent rather than when something simply goes wrong in the course of treatment and their patient is hurt. Although formal legal doctrine makes physician negligence the sine qua non of tort liability, the mismatch reported in Chapter 4 between the claims that are filed and the negligent injuries that actually occur indicates that doctors are not far off in their perception of when the litigation system is set in motion by patients and their attorneys.

Second, doctors themselves appear to seriously *under*estimate the true risk of iatrogenic injury to patients: although they inflate the chance of suit per 100 doctors by a factor of 3, they inflate the chance of suit per patient injury by a factor of 10. At least part of the explanation for the latter gap emerged from the personal interviews with physicians in which we explored a series of examples of possible medical injury and negligence. We found marked variation among physicians in their willingness to label certain kinds of medical outcomes as iatrogenic, and an even more pronounced reluctance to label as negligent those treatment decisions that, *ex post* at least, were clearly erroneous.

The physician surveys put a rather different gloss on the litigation gap disclosed in Chapter 4. Malpractice law seems to function in a manner akin to income tax audits. Only a small fraction of potentially valid malpractice claims ever ripen into lawsuits. However, doctors' inflated perceptions of the prospect of suit greatly magnify the deterrent leverage that litigation can exert over medical practice, at least by comparison with what would be expected from a simple calculation of the true statistical risk of suit.

One explanation for this physician misperception might be the psychological tendency of people to overestimate the odds of events that, albeit occasional, are highly traumatic when they do occur. That suggestion itself posed another issue for our survey: if the malpractice insurer absorbs all the costs of liability, why do doctors find the litigation experience so distasteful?

A relevant finding from our questionnaire is that in fact doctors bear some financial costs from being caught up in litigation. Doctors who had been sued reported spending a median time of 3 to 5 working days on the case; a number of doctors spent more than 20 days, and the overall average was 6 days. At roughly $1,100 in revenues lost from each potential day of practice in New York, this uninsured cost to the doctors of being sued—irrespective of ultimate disposition of the case—amounted to an average of $7,000 per claim. In addition, 6 percent of the doctors surveyed had out-of-pocket expenses from retaining their own attorney for the case, and 2 percent paid their own money to settle a claim brought by a patient.

While it was not insignificant, the direct financial burden of malpractice litigation paled by comparison with the psychological burden that our personal interviews of physicians disclosed. Doctors consistently expressed great distress, even anguish, over having their professional performance and competence attacked—perhaps even publicly stigmatized in open court—in a claim brought by a patient whom the doctor had been trying to care for. It is the personal involvement of an individual doctor in a malpractice suit that gives this litigation an emotional edge far greater than occurs, say, in product litigation over a prescription drug—litigation in which the victim's stake may be just as high, but where the people defending the claim are officials of a large corporation who are rarely accused of personal wrongdoing.

Given their special point of view, then, it is not surprising that our surveyed physicians reported that malpractice litigation had a pronounced impact on their practice patterns; yet they did not rate litigation very high as an influence for maintaining or improving the actual quality of patient treatment.

Table 6.2 presents the results of a regression analysis of our phys-

ble 6.2 Relative odds of practice changes by physician characteristics

	Outcome variable			
planatory variable	Order more tests/procedures	Explain risks	Reduce number patients/procedures	More paperwork
e (years)	1.03[a]	1.01	1.05[a]	0.98
n-HMO office practice	2.19[a]	1.28	2.10[a]	1.89[a]
it history	0.94	1.89[a]	0.66	1.44
rceived risk of suit	1.04[a]	1.42	1.01[a]	1.01

a. $p < .05$.

ician reports of changes in their practice over the last decade against the distribution of perceived risk of suit, controlling for the age, sex, location, specialty, and practice setting of the doctor. The threat of a tort suit was found to be associated with a substantially greater likelihood that doctors would order more tests or treatment procedures and would reduce the number of patients seen or modes of practice undertaken—the elimination of deliveries by obstetrician-gynecologists or of minor surgery by family practitioners. The actual experience rather than the mere perceived risk of being sued made our respondents twice as likely to take more time in explaining the risks of treatment to their patients. Interestingly, though, while spending more time on paperwork and maintaining the patient record was the change in practice most commonly reported by our surveyed physicians, this change was not associated with variations in either perceived or actual risk of suit. Greater paperwork is most likely attributable, then, to the sharply increased oversight now being exercised by hospitals, insurers, and government agencies, rather than to the prospect of doctors' having to account for their actions to juries.

Even if increased litigation generates certain kinds of defensive responses from doctors, do these responses help maintain the quality of treatment to patients? Table 6.3 presents the appraisal by our surveyed physicians of the influence of malpractice suits as compared to other institutional factors on standards of care. There was little difference in the mean scores for each factor when broken down by

Table 6.3   Factors influencing standards of care

Factor	Number responding	Mean[a]	Standard error
Continuing medical education	656	3.73	0.05
Medical journals	654	3.61	0.05
Peer relations	652	3.27	0.07
Implications of possible malpractice litigation	654	2.54	0.08
Clinical care rules, guidelines, standard operating procedures developed by clinical department and/or hospital	654	2.52	0.08
Morbidity/mortality conferences and tumor boards	652	2.33	0.07
External organized peer review, e.g., peer review organization	654	1.78	0.07

a. Scale is 1 to 5, with 5 being most important. Means are weighted to reflect differential response, as described in text.

the specialty, region, or suit status of our respondents. Clearly doctors rate highest the influence of positive reinforcement by their professional colleagues—for example, through continuing medical education, medical journals, and peer relations. They rate external review by a PRO as by far the lowest. The threat of a malpractice suit was placed somewhere between these two poles, on a par with clinical care guidelines developed in the hospital or the judgments made by the morbidity conferences and tumor boards inside the institution.

The in-depth personal interviews presented a somewhat different ordering of influences than did the broad-based written questionnaire. While admittedly not a representative sample, the physician interviewees grouped malpractice litigation together with the PRO and the state disciplinary board. The objection to all such procedures was that review of the doctor's treatment came long after the fact (several years in the case of litigation), the review was usually motivated by some factor other than the relative quality of care (such as the injured patient's need for money), and it was often carried out by people who did not enjoy great respect in the profession (in particular, the lay jury), so that both the process and the verdict had a random, lottery-like quality as far as the unlucky doctor was concerned. By contrast, hospital quality assurance programs attracted much more favorable appraisals. The reason is that reviews in such programs are reasonably concurrent with the time of treatment, they focus on the quality of treatment rather than on the eventual disability of the patient, and they are conducted by other doctors who are known and respected in the institution.

ECONOMETRIC ANALYSIS

What was disclosed by the second component of the deterrence study, the econometric analysis of what happens to patients whose treatment takes place within the law's orbit? Our best estimate, presented in Table 6.4, is that the more malpractice suits that are brought against the doctors and other providers in a particular hospital, the fewer the number of negligent medical injuries that will be suffered by patients in that hospital. Notwithstanding the efforts described earlier, however, this result did not reach the conventional level of statistical significance and thence scientific demonstration.[17]

As was evident from the earlier description of our methodological struggles with this problem, this failure is not surprising. We faced a complex array of potential causal factors that had to be sorted out in our comparatively small sample of one year's patient admissions to the 49 hospitals whose claims data seemed reliable. Not only were all these hospitals formally subject to the same tort system, but we could exploit only part of the actual variation in claims intensity across hospitals—the part that was attributable to urbanization and population density, not to the injury rate itself. Although we did observe the hypothesized relationship in our sample—the more tort claims, the fewer negligent injuries—we cannot exclude the possibility that this relationship was coincidental rather than causal.

Let us accept for the sake of policy argument the point estimate of the malpractice effect summarized in Table 6.4 for our New York sample. How would this be translated into an assessment of the preventive impact of malpractice litigation on negligent injuries?

For that exercise we preserved the Table 6.4 values for all the other

Table 6.4   Proportion of adverse events that are negligent

Variable	Coefficient	Standard error
Claims/negligent adverse event[a]	−0.37	1.97
Minority %		
0–25	1.86	1.18
25–100	−0.50	1.82
Age		
0–65	0.0023[b]	0.0008
65+	0.0049	0.0051
Hospital type (Omitted: proprietary)		
Major public	0.24	0.16
Minor public	0.17	0.37
Voluntary		
Academic medical center	0.03	0.38
Teaching affiliate	0.32[c]	0.14
Nonteaching	0.16	0.10
Black race	0.22	0.16
Payor: self or Medicaid	0.0018	0.03
DRG risk group (scaled 1–4)	−0.12[b]	0.01
Location (omitted: upstate MSA)		
Nassau County	0.33	0.61
New York City	−0.02	0.36
Upstate, non-MSA	−0.01	0.48
County per capita income	−0.00005	0.00016
Stratum dummy variable		
High-risk stratum	0.092[b]	0.026
Low-risk stratum	0.24	0.050
Intercept	−0.19	0.36

Dependent variable: whether adverse event was negligent
Estimation method: Probit
Sample size: 843
Number of positive values: 189
   a. Predicted or instrumental variable; differs from mean in Chapter 4 for reasons described in text.
   b. Significant at the 1 percent level.
   c. Significant at the 5 percent level (one-tail test).
   Note: MSA = metropolitan statistical area.

characteristics potentially influencing injury risks for patients, but hypothetically varied the actual statewide averages of malpractice claims. We found that whereas at the present claims intensity level the negligent injury rate is 0.89 percent of admissions, the patient injury risk would rise to 1.25 percent if we assumed that there were no malpractice claims activity. Similarly, whereas the overall medical injury rate in our sample is 3.3 percent of hospital admissions, this would rise to 3.7 percent if we posited a zero claims rate. Expressing these potential changes in the opposite direction, the current level of litigation intensity in New York appeared to be reducing the negligent injury rate in our sample by 29 percent (from 1.25 to 0.89) and overall medical injuries by 11 percent (from 3.7 to 3.3). We reiterate, though, that these injury prevention estimates have no more statistical significance than the point estimate from which they were translated.

Implications

The Harvard Medical Practice Study constituted the first-ever attempt to develop tangible evidence of whether malpractice litigation reduces medical injuries. We produced some indication that the answer to that question is affirmative, but the results are not conclusive from either a scientific or a policy perspective.

What is the practical significance of the fact that our tort prevention estimates did not pass the test of statistical significance? The understandable convention in the scientific community is to adopt the "null hypothesis"—that is, that there is *no* injury prevention effect of malpractice law—unless the results from the immediate sample could not have occurred by chance more than once every 20 (or 100) times. However, in the tort arena, as in other areas of public concern, lawmakers cannot wait to act until there is scientifically conclusive evidence (and there is no such evidence for the negative verdict). With respect to malpractice prevention, that scientific assurance will require the collection of medical injury and malpractice litigation data from a large national sample of hospitals over several years, so as to be able to reduce the confidence intervals around the estimated impact of variations in tort litigation. Since it took several years for us to execute such a study in New York alone, we suspect it will be a long time before such a data base is available for further econometric analysis.

In the meantime, we believe that for purposes of practical policy-making, the safest course is to accept the indication shown in Table 6.4 that malpractice litigation does have an injury prevention effect, however statistically fragile the specific point estimate might be.

- Our physician survey made it quite clear that doctors do alter their behavior in a variety of ways in response to the tangible threat posed by tort suits.
- Analysis of medical injury data discussed in Chapter 3 indicated that certain categories of patient—the elderly, the uninsured, and those treated in hospitals with predominantly minority patients—experienced a higher proportion of provider negligence in connection with the medical injuries they suffered. These are precisely the categories of patients whose ability to sue is likely to pose the lowest threat to their providers.
- Finally, our econometric analysis provides some evidence, though not scientific demonstration, that the higher the number of malpractice claims, the lower the number of negligent injuries experienced by the patient population as a whole. That result emerged from our data even though the host of constraints on the data set combined to reduce rather than enhance the likelihood that such a causal connection would manifest itself.

Indeed, some might suggest that our point estimate of the impact of tort on medical injuries is probably understated. The reason is that in order to calculate the apparent results of eliminating the liability risk, we used the injury experience in hospitals with minimal claims exposure. These hospitals and the doctors associated with them clearly faced a much smaller risk of being sued than did those in areas of the state with average litigation rates (let alone those at the 90th percentile level). Still, however low the litigation levels may have been in particular areas, everyone was still formally governed by the same malpractice legal scheme. Even in the apparently zero-risk areas, there was a real chance that suit might be brought by a patient whose negligent injury was especially severe and obvious. Consequently, if the malpractice law in New York were repealed and all providers fully insulated against suit, the predicted increase in medical injury rates would be even greater than the rate stated earlier, 11 percent. Of course, we do not know whether such an estimate would turn out to be statistically significant and scientifically conclusive.

The factor just discussed was merely one of the host of methodological hurdles we faced in trying to tease out the relationship between malpractice litigation and medical injury in our limited sample of cases. Whatever weight is given to the results of the econometric analysis, the various pieces of this part of our work still serve to put the performance of the malpractice regime in a somewhat more favorable light. However ill-suited it may be as a vehicle for delivering compensation to people who are already injured, the litigation system seems to protect many patients from being injured in the first place. And since prevention before the fact is generally preferable to compensation after the fact, the apparent injury prevention effect must be an important factor in the debate about the future of the malpractice litigation system.

Even if one ignores their scientific fragility, though, our findings are not decisive for the policy debate, for two reasons. The first is that we have not been able to determine the overall social cost of securing such an injury prevention effect. The other is that we have not considered whether, relative to other forms of medical liability, tort liability secures as much or more injury prevention, irrespective of the costs.

As part of our original econometric analysis, we tried to estimate the increased expenditures on patient care in New York associated with increases in the threat of suit. Again, however, with the limited data available to us, we were not able to derive stable and statistically significant results from that analysis.

The findings of our physician survey, however, added to the growing body of evidence that increased malpractice litigation evokes pronounced changes in doctor behavior. Combining the two features of our research on tort deterrence, our study suggests that the resulting defensive medicine should not be regarded negatively, merely as costly and unproductive measures designed only to reduce the risk of suit. Just as defensive driving avoids accidents as well as taking more time, the physician response to a higher threat of suit includes steps that appear to forestall some patient injuries as well as to increase health care costs.

How should we appraise the current balance between such added benefits and added cost? While some of the reactions of our surveyed physicians might seem intrinsically valuable—in particular, doctors' taking more time to explain to patients the consequences of different treatment options—others, such as increased tests and procedures, one would rather avoid unless they had a demonstrable benefit. Indeed, increasing the use of the health care system in this way not only adds to its financial expense—perhaps $10 billion or more a year—but can also reduce accessibility of the system to certain patients who need care but who now cannot afford it.

How can we tell when there is an "optimal" blend of added tort prevention and added medical costs? On the basis of rough back-of-the-envelope calculations, Patricia Danzon has suggested that the tort system would pay for itself if it reduced negligent injury rates by 20 percent or more.[18] That figure may include a more sizable allowance for the costs of defensive medicine than hard data would indicate, and may incorporate a smaller dollar estimate of the benefits of preventing fatal or seriously disabling injuries (the value of which is significantly higher even in economic terms than the dollar amount of tort damages awarded as compensation for such injuries after the harm has occurred). Yet even with these caveats our point estimate that negligent injuries in our sample were reduced by 29 percent would comfortably pass the Danzon test. And our injury prevention estimate is in fact likely to be low because of the assumption that areas in the state with zero litigation rates faced zero legal liability.

The results reported in this chapter persuaded us that the case for the malpractice system is somewhat stronger than one might have surmised from the results reported in Chapters 4 and 5. This does not mean that the case is decisive for the current legal scheme of imposing fault-based liability on individual doctors. There is another possible version of medical liability—strict liability imposed on the health care organization—that would certainly do a better job in terms of compensation, and promises to do at least as well, if not better, in terms of prevention. Those possibilities will be explored in the next chapter.

CHAPTER 7

Ruminations for the Future

Medical malpractice has regularly been front-page news over the last two decades. Popular and political interest was sparked not just by soaring liability premiums in the mid-1970s and the mid-1980s, but again in the summer of 1991 when President Bush unveiled his ideas for a "kinder, gentler" model of malpractice litigation. To an unfortunate extent debate about the present law and proposed alternatives to it has rested on anecdotal evidence selected to suit the self-interests and ideological commitments of the protagonists. We undertook this long and arduous empirical investigation to shed more light and hopefully less heat on the struggle over the future of medical liability.

The Harvard Study constitutes the first comprehensive investigation of all dimensions of the interplay between medical injuries and malpractice litigation—indeed, the first such study of any type of personal injury. The principal investigators in the overall study brought to the project widely divergent training and intuitive reactions to the tort system. We began with no preconceived point of view about what should be done with the malpractice system. Now, after working together for a half dozen years, we have a much stronger consensus about what our empirical findings imply for the future of legal policy in this area. In the following pages we will relate our major findings to the principal positions in the broader policy debate.

The Reform Agenda

Under the current common law a patient who is injured as a result of the fault (typically the negligent treatment) of a doctor or other provider may sue in court and ask a civil jury to award what it concludes are appropriate damages for all the losses suffered as a result of the injury. Damages may include compensation for both financial losses—medical and household expenses and lost earnings —and nonfinancial harms, including not simply the patient's immediate pain and suffering, but also long-term loss of enjoyment of life as a result of permanent disability, and the family's loss of support and companionship from the disabled patient.

Doctors argue that this system has produced spiraling and excessive levels of litigation and damage awards. Standard legislative reforms[1] seek to erect roadblocks in the way of patient claims through limits on the level of contingent fees that may now induce lawyers to undertake speculative suits, and through mandatory screening or certification procedures that require independent evaluation of the validity of a claim before a doctor is exposed to formal suit. In addition, doctors and their legislative supporters have sought to cut back on the size of damage awards, especially the occasional huge award, by offsetting against the award any amount received from loss insurance for financial harms and by placing fixed dollar caps on the total amount available for nonpecuniary harms to patient and family.

Such are the standard measures used by state legislatures to whittle away at the common law of malpractice. Disenchantment with this process of "band-aid" reform of a regime that retains its basic characteristics of fault liability and jury administration has led some people to put more fundamental alternatives on the policy agenda.

The American Medical Association, for example, seeks to dispense with the civil jury as adjudicator of doctor fault and to substitute a specialized tribunal that would be closely tied to the administration of medical discipline.[2] With respect to substantive tort law, some academics have flirted with the idea of allowing doctors and patients to avail themselves of the private contract process to avoid all the burdens of judicially mandated liability for injuries.[3] More promising in the political arena has been the proposal to substitute for tort's generous compensation of only those injuries caused by a provider's fault the payment of specified benefits to the victims of any injury, fault-induced or not. Up to now in this country, serious consideration of the no-fault idea has been confined to specified kinds of injuries (such as obstetrical injuries or a list of so-called accelerated-compensation events).[4] However, some countries, including Sweden and Finland, have adopted the no-fault model for all medical injuries.

Hazardous Medical Care

A tacit assumption running through much of the political debate about malpractice is that American patients (like the American public generally) have an inordinate propensity to bring lawsuits over imaginary injuries and illusory negligence. This tendency is said to give rise to litigation rates against doctors that contrast sharply with the kind of competent, conscientious treatment that doctors regularly provide. This popular assumption underlies one major strand in the malpractice reform program, erection of a host of barriers to unfounded litigation. The first dramatic finding of our study is that whatever may be the merits of such litigation hurdles, the underlying assumption that too many groundless malpractice suits are initiated is unfounded.

Our medical record review, corroborating the earlier California effort,[5] demonstrates that modern medical care is an inherently risky enterprise. Nearly 4 percent of hospital admissions in New York State involved a iatrogenic injury. Roughly one-quarter of these injuries, or 1 percent of all hospital admissions in the state, resulted from the negligence of a doctor or other provider.

Our definition of iatrogenic injury was very broad—any disability caused by medical management that prolonged the hospital stay by at least one day or persisted beyond the patient's release from the hospital. That definition meant that a substantial majority of the disabling injuries were judged by our reviewers to be slight. On the other hand, almost 14 percent of the medical injuries in our sample were fatal. Extrapolated to the American population as a whole, the implication is that each year 150,000 people die from, rather than in spite of, their medical treatment.

We emphasize that many of these fatalities occurred among elderly patients who suffered from serious illnesses and thus had short life expectancies when they entered the hospital. The iatrogenic injury often tended to be the tipping point for a death that probably would have occurred soon in any event. However, the number of serious and permanent disabilities occurring among patients in sound enough underlying health to survive their medical trauma was far greater than the number of such disabilities among people injured in workplace accidents, for example. In addition, the proportion of negligence among cases of serious injuries was considerably higher than the one-quarter proportion in the overall injury group—ranging from 40 to 50 percent negligence among the severe to fatal injuries.

These findings about the risks of medical injury should be interpreted carefully. A prime reason that modern medical care is so hazardous is that it so ambitiously attempts to cure the even greater hazards of nature. Many of today's procedures are extremely risky simply by virtue of their complexity. Further, such procedures are often undertaken for patients who are so sick and otherwise fragile that in an earlier era they would have been judged unsuitable for any intervention. Unfortunately, human providers will always be prone to error in managing sophisticated technology or procedures, and there is a still greater margin for unavoidable trauma from invasive medical treatment, even when the highest standards of care have been met.

A more balanced perspective also emerges from our findings regarding the distribution of injury and negligence. For example, the incidence of injury tends to be highest among surgeons, even among surgeons in the most sophisticated teaching hospitals. But this is because these doctors must deal with patients suffering the most serious illnesses, those requiring the most complicated, most invasive, riskiest medical procedures. The momentary lapse on the part of a family practitioner who forgets to ask about the patient's sensitivity to an antibiotic until the end of an interview (but before the doctor writes the prescription) has consequences far different from what ensues when a neurosurgeon has a momentary lapse of attention during an operation on a patient's brain or spinal cord. And probably because surgeons performing delicate operations are most acutely aware of the need for the highest level of care, the proportion of negligence among the injuries that did occur was significantly lower in those institutions in which state-of-the-art medicine was most likely to be practiced.

Erratic Malpractice Litigation

While we underscore the need for a balanced interpretation of the results of the hospital records review, we cannot avoid the stark picture presented of the dangers in modern medical treatment. In the comparatively brief period Americans spend in the hospital, they suffer several times the number of injuries they suffer on the job. For the last two decades, American governments and American employers have invested increasing amounts of legal and financial resources in an effort to reduce hazards in the workplace. At least as much effort is needed to protect patients from hazards in the hospital.

When we looked at actual malpractice litigation data from New York (which has among the highest litigation rates of any state) and matched actual claims brought against potential claims estimated from our patient sample, the malpractice system did not merit particularly favorable reviews. However, the verdict is quite different from the usual popular expectation. Although most of the malpractice claims filed by our patients seemed ill-founded, the mismatch only served to aggravate the huge gap between the valid claims that could be filed and those that were filed. Not too many, but rather too few suits were brought for the negligent medical injuries inflicted on patients.

On an aggregate basis, 1 malpractice claim was filed by a New York patient for every 7.5 patients who suffered a negligent injury (that is, a real tort). Because approximately 1 in 2 tort claims is ultimately paid, this means that the legal system is actually paying just 1 malpractice claim for every 15 torts inflicted in hospitals. And even when the focus is on only the most "valuable" tort claims— that is, serious injuries to patients under 70 years of age—the ratio was 1 claim paid for every 3 negligent injuries.

On the other hand, when we matched the tort claims filed by patients against our independent appraisal of their hospital records, in only one-sixth of the cases did we find positive evidence of negligent injuries in the record. We believe that in some of the cases in the overall sample we were unable to discern from the hospital record negligence that did in fact occur. The tort system, which can draw on broader sources of information, may well pick up some of these cases. Our results make it clear, however, that a substantial majority of malpractice claims filed are not based on actual provider carelessness or even iatrogenic injury.

That finding has two policy implications. One is that in its initial filing stage the tort system is even more error-prone than the medical care system. From a more charitable perspective, the process of filing and pursuing a claim actually serves as a means of discovering what happened during the medical treatment, about which the disabled patient and his or her attorney are often unable to make an accurate judgment at the onset of litigation. Research done by others has shown that the malpractice litigation process is reasonably efficient in filtering out spurious tort claims, and in deciding which suits should receive payment and how much.[6] That discovery process, though, imposes a sizable financial and emotional burden on doctors and their insurers simply by sweeping them into lawsuits that arose on account of mistaken judgments made by patients' lawyers.

This empirical demonstration of the inaccuracies of malpractice litigation at its initiation stage seems to provide strong support for imposing legal constraints on casual use of a civil justice system that can inflict real injury on an innocent doctor. However, this kind of policy tack does not address the flip side of what emerged from our injury/claims matching procedure. The fact that a substantial proportion of the total number of claims turned out to be "false positives," that is, ill-founded claims, in turn substantially increased the number of "false negatives," that is, cases in which a claim was well founded but was not made. Although we may decry the distress visited upon doctors who are the targets of unwarranted tort claims, we must be wary of letting this sympathy persuade us to adopt legal measures that could swell the already extensive ranks of deserving patients with serious bodily injuries who receive no financial redress from the legal system.[7]

In sum, our analysis of malpractice litigation data demonstrates that the problem is not a litigation surplus, but a litigation deficit. The gap between torts occurring in American hospitals and tort suits being filed in American courts is far greater than has ever been supposed.[8] But as we pointed out in Chapter 4, before deciding whether the litigation gap is a serious enough social problem to warrant remedial action, we must weigh the evidence (or lack thereof) that the admittedly burdensome malpractice system does sufficient good when it is invoked. The "goods" that we investigated were provision of compensation to patients for injuries that have already occurred and prevention of patient injuries that have not yet occurred.

Expensive Patient Insurance

Our patient survey found the compensation gap to be significantly lower than we had expected from the litigation gap. For example, when we compared patients who had suffered medical injury with a control group who had not, we found that the injured patients lost an additional 20 percent of time from work. Most of the financial costs from the overall hospital episode, then, arose from the underlying illness, not from the iatrogenic injury.

Taking a different vantage point, when we examined the potential cost of reimbursing the net financial losses of all patients who suffered more than modest disabling injuries from their medical treatment, non-negligent as well as negligent, the amount calculated was approximately $900 million for patients injured in New York State in 1984. Even after allowance was made for substantial administrative expenses, this cost turned out to be not much greater than the annual cost of malpractice insurance in New York (well over $1 billion), which compensates just a small fraction of the most seriously injured patients—indeed, only a fraction of the losses of negligently injured patients, who bore a disproportionate share of the total losses in our patient sample.

This finding provides graphic testimony in support of critics of the tort system who lament how much money is used up in litigation expenses, principally on fees paid to lawyers acting for the two sides. Furthermore, of the money that actually reaches injured patients, most is spent on reimbursing financial expenses already covered by other insurance or in trying to make up in dollars for pain and suffering experienced by the victim years earlier. If the object is to channel insurance dollars toward the most important needs of injured victims, malpractice litigation seems to get a failing grade. Therein lies the appeal of proposals for compensating medical accident victims irrespective of provider fault, including New York State's new proposal for the victims of obstetrical accidents, or the Massachusetts Medical Association's proposal for compensating the victims of any kind of medical accident.[9]

Effective Injury Prevention

A no-fault system clearly scores better than tort-fault as a provider of rational and economic compensation for iatrogenic injury victims. Nevertheless, no-fault is less effective than explicit loss insurance, public or private, in performing that role. As a matter of principle, why should health care expenses and lost wages be reimbursed for patients who happen to suffer an injury in the hospital when we do not guarantee the same coverage for all sick patients going into the hospital in the first place? From the point of view of practical administration, accident insurance that is targeted at a particular category of medical accident victims requires tough decisions about the true cause of patients' current disabilities. For example, is a child's cerebral palsy the result of a difficult delivery or of some congenital condition? Although our research revealed that decisions about injury causation could be made with much greater confidence than decisions about provider negligence, there remained an irreducible fraction, roughly 5 percent, of close calls regarding medical causation. In a no-fault setting this percentage would be applicable to a considerably larger body of claimants than it is now under fault-based malpractice litigation.

A possible justification for confining the scope of no-fault patient compensation to medically caused disabilities is that doing so would allocate the legal and financial burden for such disabling injuries to the responsible actors and activities. That, in turn, might provide appropriate incentives for effective prevention of future injuries, an objective that is generally considered to be at least as important as the goal of compensating prior injuries. Certainly by comparison with current versions of the no-fault model, the major advantage of the malpractice system is that it focuses liability on those providers who were at fault in medical accidents and who were thus presumably in the best position to alter their risky behavior.

However, critics of malpractice law regularly assert that the threat of legal liability provides a very small positive return. They argue that too few cases are brought, that the cases which are brought are often the wrong ones, and that even the appropriate cases ultimately impose their burdens not on the negligent provider but on the liability insurer. Further, they maintain that the weaknesses of malpractice litigation do not create a serious social problem because sufficient incentives (ethical, market, and disciplinary) are generated within the health care system for high-quality treatment of patients.

The final leg of our research casts doubt on this critique of malpractice prevention. On the "input" side, our physician surveys demonstrated that although only a fraction of potentially litigable claims are actually filed, doctors systematically overestimate their risk of being sued. Further, although they are insured for the cost of legal liability, doctors still bear substantial uninsured costs when they are sued. Some of these costs are financial; some, perhaps the most taxing, are psychological.

Notwithstanding the considerable chance of groundless litigation, the risk of suit turns out to be substantially greater when there is a valid basis for the claim. As a result, changes that doctors reported to us in their practice behavior were strongly correlated with variations in the tort threat posed to these doctors.

As we observed earlier, malpractice litigation seems to function somewhat like an income tax audit. Only a small proportion of potential cases are singled out for scrutiny; although the targets of this unpleasant experience are too often innocent, the risk is much greater for the error-prone; finally, the costs imposed by the process are great enough to motivate significant changes in behavior designed to avoid running afoul of the law.

But it would still be useful to know whether such defensive medicine actually results in fewer patient injuries. Having assembled data on both medical injuries in our sample hospitals and malpractice claims against the same hospitals, we were able to mount the first investigation of that issue. However, we realized that formidable statistical barriers stood in the way of successfully isolating any preventive effect in our limited sample. The findings reported in

Chapter 3, that elderly, minority, and uninsured patients—people who are less likely to sue—suffer more negligent injuries, along with the negative (though not statistically significant) relationship depicted in Table 6.4 between suits and injuries, provide suggestive evidence on that score. After devoting a great deal of thought and effort to this inquiry, our best judgment is that the threat of malpractice suits does somewhat reduce the risk of patient injury. On the basis of the point estimate discussed in Chapter 6, taken at face value, the current intensity of tort litigation in New York appears to be reducing the aggregate injury rate there by approximately 10 percent.

A Future Path for Medical Liability

The prevention issue is crucial to the debate about the future of medical liability. To the extent that the present malpractice system produces a tangible reduction in the number of medical injuries, this should give real pause to those who back "reform" packages that whittle away at victims' tort rights, and especially those who suggest dismantling the entire liability regime without putting anything in its place. Proponents of no-fault insurance do advocate substituting their more sensible mode of after-the-fact compensation for victims of medical injuries. They will, however, have difficulty in persuading people that one should dispense with the contribution malpractice litigation can make toward preventing medical injuries from occurring in the first place.

This is not to deny that a forceful case can be made for reforms that enhance the productivity and predictability of the existing tort system, a topic that some of us have written about at length elsewhere.[10] But the bedrock principle must be that if malpractice is to be retained as a device for both compensating and preventing medical injuries, then any reforms adopted must not hinder access of patients to this system of redress nor weaken the incentives offered to providers for careful, high-quality treatment.

Having come to the view that *some* legal liability for medical injury is preferable to *no* liability, we must still determine *which* mode of liability is to be preferred. Should we retain existing *fault-based* tort liability, under which the focus of litigation is on the personal negligence of individual doctors? Or should we move toward broader *strict* liability imposed on the hospital, HMO, or other institution for all accidents that befall its patients, whether or not a particular injury is attributable to some individual's demonstrated carelessness?

Our research findings provide persuasive support for use in the health care field of the workers' compensation model, which imposes strict liability on employers for occupational injuries befalling their employees.[11] As compared with tort law, at least, paying specified benefits to victims irrespective of an actor's fault is a more rational form of compensation. Equally important, expanding the scope of legal liability for injuries could materially enhance the leverage now exerted by the law to secure more effective injury prevention measures within the medical care system.

Addressing the compensation side first, we believe that the hypothetical no-fault scheme we devised and costed-out for New York makes far more sense as a system of loss insurance.

- Rather than providing full compensation for the losses of only a few accident victims—including damages for virtually all imaginable forms of pain and suffering—our scheme would give priority to the tangible financial losses of all injured patients, the types of loss that insurance theory and practice demonstrate are best suited for such redress.
- Rather than serving as first-dollar primary insurance for all the financial losses of just a handful of successful tort claimants, our no-fault plan would concentrate liability dollars on victims of longer-term injuries who do not enjoy protection for these more catastrophic losses from other sources of medical and disability insurance. In this respect, the system would function analogously to the collateral source offset provision that has now emerged in the malpractice regimes in a number of states, including New York.
- Rather than conditioning receipt of benefits on the outcome of a long, expensive, emotionally draining contest between doctor and patient over whether the doctor was professionally culpable in the care delivered, our plan would compensate a patient simply upon a determination that the injury was iatrogenic, a process in which the patient's doctor might occasionally play a helpful rather than adversarial role.

It was evident from analysis of the hospital records in New York that in certain kinds of cases it can be extremely difficult to make a connection between the treatment and the subsequent disability. In the aggregate, however, only a small fraction (5 percent) of our reviewers' causal judgments were labeled close calls: in contrast, the proportion of difficult negligence judgments in our sample was four times greater. Both the experience with no-fault patient compensation in other countries such as Sweden, and the experience under no-fault workers' compensation in this country, testify to the huge savings in social and legal resources that could be realized by focusing solely on medical causation rather than on both causation and negligence, as is required under the present tort regime.

Contrary to the beliefs of many commentators, our work shows that we can afford such carefully targeted, readily accessible insurance for the high-priority needs of all seriously injured medical accident victims. The basis for that fiscal judgment appears obvious upon comparing the likely cost of no-fault with the overall health care budget, of which such disability insurance would be only a tiny fraction. (Moreover, a significant part of such compensation would serve to pay for expensive treatment in the same health care system.) However, no-fault compensation for all medical accident victims even seems affordable by comparison to the present malpractice insurance bill, a bill that is likely to take another upward leap in the 1990s as it has in the past two decades.

Yet it is crucial to avoid focusing simply on the problem of compensation after the fact and thereby risk diluting the incentives directed by the legal system against careless medical practice before the fact. That is precisely the mistake made by the designers of the no-fault obstetrical accident schemes enacted (in very narrow versions) in Virginia and Florida and proposed (on a somewhat broader basis) for New York State. In each of these programs, although financial responsibility for the insurance funds resides within the overall health care system, the burden is diffused among all doctors and hospitals who contribute to this mandatory fund. What we envisage instead is imposing a form of strict liability on the particular hospital or other institution responsible for the treatment of the patient who was injured. That organization would consequently be motivated to use the many devices available to it to ensure that its own doctors, nurses, and other providers adhere to the appropriate level of care for their patients.

Recent studies of workers' compensation provide striking evidence that the preventive effect this kind of liability model exerts on occupational injuries is considerably stronger and statistically more robust than the preventive effect that the current medical malpractice system has on iatrogenic injuries.[12] For several reasons we expect that the preventive effect of employing strict liability in the medical setting, where we have shown the present risk of injury to be far higher than it is in the workplace, would be at least equally powerful.

First, with respect to the comparatively few medical injuries that are now compensated under tort law—that is, the very small fraction of cases in which a doctor's fault is demonstrated through litigation —legal responsibility would still be imposed under our proposed strict liability system. Of course, the size of any one damage award would typically be more modest than the magnitude of damages paid under the current open-ended regime of tort damages for both financial losses and pain and suffering. However, offsetting that fact are two marked advantages under strict liability.

One advantage is that many more victims of iatrogenic injuries would be compensated for the losses that result from the injuries. Our research showed that currently only a tiny fraction of negligently injured patients—usually the most seriously injured—ever realize on their tort right to compensation for these injuries. The legal system is likely to become much more accessible even to victims of fault-caused injury if they do not have to identify and prove such fault to the satisfaction of a jury, against the stiff resistance of doctors trying to avoid being publicly labeled as negligent in their professional practice.

The other advantage is that the burden of paying for the more numerous but somewhat smaller awards would be imposed on the particular health care institution in which the substandard care took place. This cost allocation would contrast with the present malpractice regime. On its face the legal system now imposes responsibility on the individual doctor who was negligent, but the award is actually paid from a pool of non-merit-rated malpractice insurance. Under this arrangement the addition of more claims and awards against a few doctors who are adjudged careless serves only to raise the premiums of all doctors in the particular specialty or region. By contrast, organizationally based strict liability would utilize either self-insurance or heavily experience-rated insurance; consequently, any institution in which more injuries occurred would bear a correspondingly higher financial burden. That burden would in turn generate an incentive for the hospital to look for patterns of injury causation that might offer some prospect of management and control. At a minimum, hospital management could be expected to monitor and control more closely the practice privileges of physicians who were more prone to negligent accidents. More-sophisticated organizations would be motivated to follow the example of the Harvard teaching hospitals in the anesthesia field, to develop and install fail-safe devices that would guard against the injurious effects of errors, which are inevitable on the part of even the best physicians.[13]

The comparative advantages of strict liability over fault-based liability are pronounced even in the case of fault-caused medical accidents. Equally important from a prevention point of view are our findings that only one-quarter of all medical injuries and one-half of seriously disabling or fatal injuries were due to negligence. The virtue of the strict liability model is that rather than contracting, it sharply expands the scope of legal responsibility for medical injury.

A predictable rejoinder is that such an extension of liability cannot prevent injuries that occur absent some individual's discernible fault. If an injury could not have been avoided by reasonable precautions, what prevention value is served by imposing on the health care provider a liability incentive to avoid the unavoidable?

The fallacy in this challenge is its static perspective on the medical accident problem. Present malpractice law confines itself to enforcing what the medical profession adopts as its customary procedures and precautions according to the current state of the art. But the medical art is constantly evolving under the impetus of newly developed diagnostic and treatment techniques and equipment. Many injuries that were considered unavoidable but acceptable risks at one time become readily avoidable and unacceptable just a few years later. For example, a mortality rate of 10 percent or higher used to characterize the pioneering open-heart surgery programs in the best teaching hospitals; but a rate this high would now trigger radical changes in personnel and procedures in any institution in which it was observed. The special virtue of a strict liability regime that extends its reach to all medical injuries is that this regime directs a continual, nonmoralistic incentive at the health care system to invest in research and innovation in safer medical techniques. That is a vital advantage, given our finding that iatrogenic injury is a serious risk for all patients who submit themselves to the procedures of modern high-technology medicine.[14]

An Experimental Approach

The foregoing represents the argument for adopting the strict liability model for medical injuries. The findings of the Harvard Medical Practice Study provide persuasive support at key points in that argument. We have not, however, empirically demonstrated the comparative virtues of the no-fault approach we envisage, for the simple reason that there is no existing version of this model that we can study and compare.

We also acknowledge certain legitimate concerns about how no-fault might fare in operation, concerns in the same compensatory, administrative, and preventive areas in which we measured the shortcomings of the tort-fault system. For example, although the size of compensable losses might appear tolerable in New York, one of the highest malpractice cost states in the nation, it might be less so in states in which draconian statutory caps have kept malpractice premiums artificially low. (Even in those states the cost of patient compensation would be only a small fraction of the total health care budget.) In New York, meanwhile, there would be understandable fear that our estimates of the costs of compensating the true victims of serious medical injuries do not allow for a probable influx of marginal cases filed to take advantage of the new benefits. (However, as we noted earlier, there would also be a considerable number of medically injured patients who would not realize that they had valid claims against this program.)

These concerns on the cost and compensation side underscore the evident difficulties of claims administration. Such difficulties consist not just of the practical challenge of untangling the disabling effects of a medical injury from the underlying illness, but also of the conceptual problems in staking out the boundaries of a medical accident regime. For example, as we explained at the outset of Chapter 3, pure no-fault compensation for medical injury is not possible, because one crucial category of medical causation, the failure to diagnose or select the proper treatment for a disabling or fatal disease, often turns on a judgment about whether the doctor took appropriate steps in the case—that is, whether the doctor displayed reasonable care in diagnosis and treatment.

Another set of medical injuries results from the interplay of health care providers and the manufacturers of prescription drugs or therapeutic equipment. Experience in the world of occupational injuries testifies to the difficulties in establishing the proper boundary between a patient's claim lodged under medical no-fault against providers and a companion claim lodged by the same patient for the same incident against a product manufacturer governed by tort law.[15]

Although no-fault patient insurance poses such administrative difficulties, we can draw upon considerable experience in other quarters for possible solutions. With respect to prevention, though, trial lawyers will lodge strong objections to eliminating the moral incentive that supposedly inheres in holding individual doctors publicly responsible for their faulty behavior. Ironically, that objection occurs in tandem with resistance on the part of many doctors to the idea that their personal treatment decisions would be monitored and occasionally constrained by the hospital administration. (We do note, parenthetically, that there are some doctors who are not affiliated with any health care institution that would bear responsibility for their patients under this strict liability program.) Finally, economists in particular worry about the problem of adverse selection: that hospitals held liable for any injury to their patients will adopt measures to screen out (or "dump") patients who pose a high risk of injury, rather than simply adopt more effective precautions against the injury.

We have candidly spelled out these concerns about strict medical liability, and we believe that there are ways of addressing each of them. Of course, the bottom-line question is not whether no-fault would be imperfect (surely it would be), but whether society would fare better with this system than with the evidently flawed regime of malpractice litigation.

Still, we empathize with state legislators who are loath to take a leap in the dark by repealing the malpractice system in one fell swoop and substituting mandatory strict liability across the board. Even ignoring the severe political obstacles posed by those strange bedfellows, the American Medical Association and the American Trial Lawyers Association, we are not sure that this is the best scenario to follow. We are attracted, instead, to a different approach: enacting legislation that would facilitate adoption of the strict liability model on an incremental elective basis.[16] Few people remember that precisely the same path was followed early in this century in the gradual emergence of strict workers' compensation liability for occupational injuries.

We visualize the following approach:

- A statute would be enacted that explicitly empowered hospitals and other health care organizations to offer their patients administrative compensation for iatrogenic injuries in return for a waiver of the common-law tort liability of the hospital and its providers.
- The legislation would require that benefits payable meet certain standards of generosity, including full out-of-pocket medical expenses (that is, those not covered by direct insurance), 80 percent of net lost earnings up to 200 percent of the state's average earnings level, plus specified payments for loss of enjoyment of life associated with certain physical impairments.
- The claims administration procedure would meet acceptable standards of accessibility, neutrality, and due process.
- The program would cover all injuries inflicted on the hospital's patients, even those caused by nonemployee doctors with admitting privileges to the hospital, and even those caused by diagnostic or treatment decisions made in the doctors' offices.
- Appropriate adjustments would be made in the revenues received for their services by all participants, both in fees paid to the hospitals shouldering this new strict liability, and to the doctors being relieved of personal tort liability.[17]
- The health care facility would have to operate an effective quality assurance program that would include internal measures for assessing accountability for medical injuries identified through this claims process. State immunity from antitrust liability would cover the doctor-members of hospital peer review committees that suspend the practice privileges of accident-prone physicians.
- Patients would have to be fully informed in easily comprehensible terms of both the tort rights they were surrendering and the no-fault benefits they would be eligible to receive, before they were

asked to decide either to accept medical care under no-fault auspices or to use institutions and doctors still governed by the existing tort regime.

This scenario for reform offers several important advantages. The most obvious is that it is much easier to offer doctors and their patients a choice about no-fault, a choice made under carefully tailored protection, than to convince the general public (including the medical community) to mandate no-fault for everyone. Next, elective no-fault affords us the chance to learn from the experience of pioneer institutions blazing this trail: to observe, for example, how these institutions deal with issues such as whether it is best to specify one kind of designated event as compensable or not,[18] or whether a certain type of fringe benefit (for example, lost employer contributions to a pension plan) should be compensable earnings or not. Finally, careful scientific study of such demonstration projects, monitored as they operate side by side with the tort-fault system, would enable everyone realistically to appreciate the comparative advantages and disadvantages of each. That last value is especially important for those who believe, as we do, that governments should know something about the real world of medical injury and malpractice litigation before they enact reforms that profoundly affect the fates of patients, doctors, and lawyers for decades to come.

NOTES

INDEX

Notes

1. The Malpractice Setting

1. See Paul C. Weiler, *Medical Malpractice on Trial* 2, 167 (Cambridge, Mass.: Harvard University Press, 1991).

2. See the Report of the American Medical Association/Specialty Society Medical Liability Project, *A Proposed Alternative to the Civil Justice System for Resolving Medical Liability Disputes: A Fault-Based Administrative System* (Chicago: AMA, 1987).

3. American Law Institute Reporters' Study, *Enterprise Responsibility for Personal Injury* (Philadelphia: ALI, 1991) (Paul Weiler served as Chief Reporter for this ALI project).

4. Unless otherwise indicated, the statistics for New York presented in this chapter are drawn from chapter 1 of the first report of the Harvard Medical Practice Study, "Patients, Doctors, and Lawyers: Medical Injury, Malpractice Litigation, and Patient Compensation in New York" (Cambridge, Mass: Harvard University, 1990) (hereafter Harvard Study), and statistics for other states or for the nation as a whole are drawn from Weiler, *Medical Malpractice on Trial.* Extensive references can be found in those earlier works of members of the Harvard Study team for the assertions we make here about the background to the research reported in this book.

5. Detailed documentation of this fact in the case of Florida (whose premium levels are as high as New York's) can be found in David J. Nye, Donald G. Gifford, Bernard L. Webb, and Marvin A. Dewar, "The Causes of the Medical Malpractice Crisis: An Analysis of Claims Data and Insurance Company Finances," 76 *Georgetown Law Journal* 1495 (1988).

6. See Report of the New York State Insurance Department on Medical Malpractice, *A Balanced Prescription for Change* 68–74 (Albany, 1988).

7. New York Department of Health, *Monitoring Health Care Quality* (Albany, 1988), appendix B.

8. Frank A. Sloan, Paula M. Mergenhagen, W. Bradley Burfield, Randall R. Bovbjerg, and Mahmud Hassan, "Medical Malpractice Experience of Physicians: Predictable or Haphazard?" 262 *Journal of the American Medical Association* 3291 (1989). See to the same effect John E. Rolph, Richard L. Kravitz, and Kimberly McGuigan, "Malpractice Claims Data as a Quality Improvement Tool. II. Is Targeting Effective?" 266 *Journal of the American Medical Association* 2093 (1991).

9. With respect to New York, the details of these legislative changes are presented in New York State Insurance Department on Medical Malpractice, *A Balanced Prescription for Change;* and in Association of the Bar of the City of New York Ad Hoc Committee on Medical Malpractice, *Report on Recommendations for the State of New York* (New York, 1988). In-depth reviews of malpractice legislation across the country in the 1970s and 1980s respectively can be found in Glen O. Robinson, "The Medical Malpractice Crisis of the 1970's: A Retrospective," 49 *Law and Contemporary Problems* 5 (1986); and Randall R. Bovbjerg, "Legislation on Medical Malpractice: Further Developments and a Preliminary Report Card," 22 *U.C. Davis Law Review* 499 (1989). See also Weiler, *Medical Malpractice on Trial,* chap. 2.

10. See Patricia M. Danzon, "The Frequency and Severity of Medical Malpractice Claims: New Evidence," 49 *Law and Contemporary Problems* 57 (1986); and Frank A. Sloan, Paula M. Mergenhagen, and Randall R. Bovbjerg, "Effects of Tort Reforms on the Value of Closed Medical Malpractice Claims: A Microanalysis," 14 *Journal of Health Politics, Policy, and Law* 663 (1989).

11. The probable explanation is the fact that malpractice damage awards are so high. Recently Randall R. Bovbjerg, Frank A. Sloan, Avi Dor, and Chee Ruey Hsieh, "Juries and Justice: Are Malpractice and Other Personal Injuries Created Equal?" 54 *Law and Contemporary Problems* 5 (1991), found that even with age, degree of physical impairment, economic loss, and other relevant factors controlled for, medical malpractice awards were three times as high as in motor vehicle cases, twice as high as in government torts, and slightly higher even than in product litigation. The other side of the coin, though, was that the patient-victim's chances of winning a malpractice verdict was three-quarters that of the product victim, two-thirds that of the government victim, and just half that of the motor vehicle victim.

2. The Policy Debate about Medical Malpractice

1. A much larger treatment of this subject, with extensive references to the literature, is contained in Paul C. Weiler, *Medical Malpractice on Trial* (Cambridge, Mass.: Harvard University Press, 1991).

2. In the medical field, the source of a medical accident may be not only the doctor treating the patient, but also the nurse or the many other actors within the health care system, as well as the variety of organizational procedures that are not attributable to any one individual. For convenience' sake in this book, however, we generally use *doctor* as a shorthand reference to all such providers,

personal or organizational, whose medical management may contribute to patient injuries.

3. The most systematic contemporary analysis of tort law as a mode of corrective justice is contained in the writings of Ernest J. Weinrib; see his "Toward a Moral Theory of Negligence Law," in Michael D. Bayles and Bruce Chapman, eds., *Justice, Rights, and Tort Law* 123 (Boston: D. Reidel Publishing, 1983), and "Understanding Tort Law," 23 *Valparaiso University Law Review* 485 (1989).

4. A comprehensive review of this deterrence rationale for tort litigation in the medical arena is to be found in Peter A. Bell, "Legislative Intrusions into the Common Law of Medical Malpractice: Thoughts about the Deterrent Effect of Tort Liability," 35 *Syracuse Law Review* 939 (1984).

5. For a lengthy statement of this view about the tort system as a whole, see Stephen D. Sugarman, "Doing Away with Tort Law," 73 *California Law Review* 558 (1985); and to much the same effect about medical malpractice litigation itself, see Walter Gellhorn, "Medical Malpractice Litigation (U.S.)—Medical Mishap Compensation (N.Z.)," 73 *Cornell Law Review* 170 (1988).

6. Recent expositions of this critical perspective on the current principles of tort damages include Patricia M. Danzon, "Tort Reform and the Role of Government in Private Insurance Markets," 13 *Journal of Legal Studies* 517 (1984); and George L. Priest, "The Current Insurance Crisis in Modern Tort Law," 96 *Yale Law Journal* 1521 (1987). The underlying theoretical model is developed in Philip J. Cook and Daniel A. Graham, "The Demand for Insurance and Protection: The Case of Irreplaceable Commodities," 91 *Quarterly Journal of Economics* 143 (1977).

7. Indeed, in those jurisdictions that, unlike New York, have not reversed the collateral source rule, the successful tort plaintiff may well recover considerably more than full compensation for certain loss items.

8. For that reason, the profession has recently proposed replacement of civil jury trials in malpractice actions with a proceeding in front of a revamped medical licensing board: see American Medical Association/Specialties Society Medical Liability Project, *A Fault-Based Administrative System: A Proposed Alternative to the Civil Justice System for Resolving Medical Liability Disputes* (Chicago: AMA, 1987).

9. See James S. Kakalik and Nicholas M. Pace, *Costs and Compensation Paid in Tort Litigation* (Santa Monica, Calif.: RAND Institute for Civil Justice, 1986).

10. The tort system's assumptions about its ability to meaningfully influence and control the level of attention of individual actors is criticized in Howard R. Latin, "Problem-Solving Behavior and Theories of Tort Liability," 73 *California Law Review* 677 (1985); and Mark F. Grady, "Why Are People Negligent? Technology, Nondurable Precautions, and the Medical Malpractice Explosion," 82 *Northwestern University Law Review* 293 (1988), the latter focusing specifically on the medical accident setting.

11. For a description and appraisal, see Linda Darling, "The Applicability of Experience Rating to Medical Malpractice Insurance," 38 *Case Western Reserve Law Review* 254 (1987).

12. For an analysis of the sophisticated experience rating program in no-fault

workers' compensation insurance, see Richard B. Victor, *Workers' Compensation and Workplace Safety: The Nature of Employer Financial Incentives* (Santa Monica, Calif.: RAND Institute for Civil Justice, 1982).

13. See generally Bell, "Legislative Intrusions," as well as Chapter 6 here.

14. For an attempt to measure the defensive (though not necessarily the wasteful) reaction of doctors to present-day malpractice litigation, see Roger A. Reynolds, John A. Rizzo, and Martin L. Gonzales, "The Cost of Medical Professional Liability," 257 *Journal of the American Medical Association* 276 (1987).

15. For an exploration of the pros and cons of this possibility, see Glen O. Robinson, "Rethinking the Allocation of Malpractice Risk between Patients and Providers," 49 *Law and Contemporary Problems* 173 (Spring 1987); and Patrick S. Atiyah, "Medical Malpractice and the Contract/Tort Boundary," ibid. 287.

16. See, e.g., Sugarman, "Doing Away with Tort Law."

17. See, e.g., Clark C. Havighurst and Laurence Tancredi, "Medical Adversity Insurance—A No-Fault Approach to Medical Malpractice and Quality Assurance," 613 *Insurance Law Journal* 69 (1974); and Jeffrey O'Connell, "No-Fault Insurance for Injuries Arising from Medical Treatment: A Proposal for Elective Coverage," 24 *Emory Law Journal* 21 (1975).

18. For a detailed description of the New Zealand system written for an American audience, see Gellhorn, "Medical Malpractice Litigation (U.S.)—Medical Mishap Compensation (N.Z.)."

19. Specifics of the design and operation of the Swedish program are set out in Marilynn M. Rosenthal, *Dealing with Medical Malpractice: The British and Swedish Experience* 131–206 (Durham, N.C.: Duke University Press, 1988); and in Carl Oldertz, "The Swedish Patient Insurance System—Eight Years of Experience," 52 *Medical-Legal Journal* 43 (1983).

20. For the comparable trends in Canada, see Donald Dewees, Peter Coyte, and Michael Trebilcock, *Canadian Medical Malpractice Liability: An Empirical Analysis of Recent Trends* (Toronto: University of Toronto, 1989); and in the United Kingdom, see Chris Ham, Robert Dingwall, Paul Fenn, and Don Harris, *Medical Negligence: Compensation and Accountability* (Oxford: Centre for Socio-Legal Studies, 1988).

21. See Diana Brahams, "No-Fault Compensation Finnish Style," *The Lancet* 733 (Sept. 24, 1988).

22. See British Medical Association, *No-Fault Compensation Working Party Report* (London: BMA, 1987).

23. See J. Robert S. Prichard (Chairman), *Liability and Compensation in Health Care* (Toronto: University of Toronto Press, 1990).

24. For a detailed description of the background to and design of the Virginia program, upon which the Florida provision is largely modeled, see Note, "Innovative No-Fault Tort Reform for an Endangered Specialty," 74 *Virginia Law Review* 1487 (1988).

25. Useful expositions of the case that can be made for different versions of

medical no-fault are to be found in Gellhorn, "Medical Malpractice Litigation (U.S.)—Medical Mishap Compensation (N.Z.)"; and in Randall R. Bovbjerg, Laurence Tancredi, and Daniel S. Gaylin, "Obstetrics and Malpractice: Evidence on the Performance of a Selective No-Fault System," 265 *Journal of the American Medical Association* 2836 (1991).

26. This is the gist of the argument of Sugarman, "Doing Away with Tort Law," against the no-fault as well as the tort-fault model of liability as a system of victim compensation.

27. See, e.g., Robert E. Keeton, "Compensation for Medical Accidents," 121 *University of Pennsylvania Law Review* 590 (1973); and Guido Calabresi, "The Problem of Malpractice: Trying to Round Out the Circle," 27 *University of Toronto Law Journal* 131 (1977). A succinct statement of the standard current arguments against medical no-fault is presented in Patricia M. Danzon, *Medical Malpractice: Theory, Evidence, and Public Policy* 152–158 (Cambridge, Mass.: Harvard University Press, 1985).

28. California Medical Association, *Medical Insurance Feasibility Study,* ed. Donald H. Mills (San Francisco: Sutter Publications, 1977). The nature and results of this pioneering research are described in more detail in Chapter 3.

29. Ronald Conley and John Noble, "Workers' Compensation Reform: Challenge for the 80s," 1 *Research Report of the Interdepartmental Workers Compensation Task Force* 1, 57 (Washington D.C.: U.S. Government Printing Office, 1979).

30. Michael J. Moore and W. Kip Viscusi, *Compensation Mechanisms for Job Risks: Wages, Workers' Compensation, and Product Liability* 151–178 (Princeton: Princeton University Press, 1990), estimate that the incentives generated by today's experience-rated workers' compensation programs have spurred American employers to additional safety precautions that have reduced workplace fatality rates by more than 25 percent from what they would otherwise be.

31. Joseph P. Newhouse, "Do Unprofitable Patients Face Access Problems?" *Health Care Financing Review* 11 (1989).

32. This has been the consistent finding of a growing body of research about the economic effects of permanently disabling injuries to employees in the workplace: see generally Monroe Berkowitz and John F. Burton, Jr., *Permanent Disability Benefits in Workers' Compensation* (Kalamazoo: W. E. Upjohn Institute for Employment, 1987).

33. A latent effect of the current method of paying for tort litigation through the contingency fee is that the tort system also screens out the majority of smaller patient injuries and losses because these cases cannot produce an award amount, and thence a legal fee, that would warrant the up-front costs and risks involved in filing and pursuing a tort claim.

34. Nearly 60 percent of the medical malpractice claims dollar is now expended on administration in order to get just 40 percent into the injured patient's hands: see Kakalik and Pace, *Costs and Compensation Paid in Tort Litigation.*

35. See Priest, "The Current Insurance Crisis in Modern Tort Law," p. 1560.

These data for WC insurance costs, like those for tort liability insurance, do not include the business cost of selling the insurance, collecting and investing the premiums, and so on, and focus instead just on the costs of dispute resolution in distributing among victims the insurance funds thus raised.

36. See Gellhorn, "Medical Malpractice Litigation (U.S.)—Medical Mishap Compensation (N.Z.)"; and Rosenthal, *The British and Swedish Experience.*

37. See Moore and Viscusi, *Compensation Mechanisms for Job Risks,* pp. 151–178. As well, the Swedish no-fault patient compensation scheme has recently turned its attention to the issue of prevention. Its entire body of case claims and payments is now being mined as a data base for research that isolates certain settings and procedures that are especially prone to iatrogenic injuries and then devises alternative, less risky practice protocols that are reported in Swedish medical journals; see Rosenthal, *The British and Swedish Experience,* pp. 184–186.

3. The Epidemiology of Medical Injury

1. With regard to negligence, we used a modified "locality" standard similar to that employed by peer review organizations: see Timothy Jost, "Administrative Law Issues Involving the Medicare Utilization and Quality Control Peer Review Organization (PRO) Program: Analysis and Recommendations," 50 *Ohio State Law Journal* 1 (1989). For example, physicians in small rural hospitals may be constrained by the resources available to them. While we followed the lead of common-law developments eroding the so-called locality rule, we did not require that a reviewer imagine that all the resources of, say, a tertiary-care teaching hospital were available at small community hospitals.

2. See Harvard Study, chap. 5; and Paul C. Weiler, *Medical Malpractice on Trial* (Cambridge, Mass.: Harvard University Press, 1991), pp. 139–144.

3. The Medical Insurance Feasibility Study, as it was called, was commissioned by the California Medical and Hospital Associations to obtain information about the extent of medical injuries in order, among other reasons, to test the feasibility of no-fault compensation for such injuries. See California Medical Association, *Medical Insurance Feasibility Study,* ed. Donald H. Mills (San Francisco: Sutter Publications, 1977).

4. The few other studies of iatrogenic injuries also suffer from these methodological problems, and in addition involve sample sizes too small to be readily generalizable: see Knight Steel et al., "Iatrogenic Illness on a General Medical Service at a University Hospital," 304 *New England Journal of Medicine* 638 (1981); Nathan Couch et al., "The High Cost of Low-Frequency Events: The Anatomy and Economics of Surgical Mishaps," 304 *New England Journal of Medicine* 634 (1981); Mark C. Lakshamanan et al., "Hospital Admissions Caused by Iatrogenic Disease," 146 *Archives of Internal Medicine* 1931 (1986).

5. The screening criteria are listed and explained in Troyen A. Brennan et al., "Identification of Adverse Events Occurring during Hospitalization: A Cross-

Sectional Study of Litigation, Quality Assurance, and Medical Records at Two Teaching Hospitals," 112 *Annals of Internal Medicine* 221 (1990).

6. See Troyen A. Brennan et al., "Reliability and Validity of Judgments concerning Adverse Events Suffered by Hospitalized Patients," 27 *Medical Care* 1148 (1989).

7. See Robert Dubois and Robert H. Brook, "Preventable Death: Who, How Often, and Why?" 110 *Annals of Internal Medicine* 582 (1988).

8. See, e.g., Lisa Rubenstein et al., "Changes in Quality of Care for Five Diseases Measured by Implicit Review, 1981 to 1986," 264 *Journal of the American Medical Association* 1974 (1990).

9. See Brennan et al., "Reliability and Validity," p. 1148.

10. See Brennan et al., "Identification of Adverse Events," p. 221.

11. Outpatient records themselves rarely demonstrate evidence of an adverse event. The California study reviewed 928 outpatient records and found only 2 minor adverse events: see California Medical Association, *Medical Insurance Feasibility Study*, p. 45.

12. Our survey design was facilitated by the fact that New York maintains a statewide planning and research cooperative system (SPARCS), a computerized file with information for all patient discharges from hospitals in the state. This provided us with general demographic information on all hospitals and all 2.7 million individuals discharged from acute care, nonpsychiatric New York hospitals in 1984.

13. For a more detailed discussion, see Harvard Study, chap. 4.

14. In particular, we randomly chose four hospitals to undertake a complete review of missing records. We identified 154 of 326 missing records, or 47.2 percent, in the follow-up visits to these hospitals. The adverse event rate in these new files was 2.5 percent, while the negligence rate was 0.7 percent.

15. Harvard Study, pp. 9–15.

16. The findings reported here are derived from Chapter 6 of the *Harvard Study* and from subsequent papers by Troyen A. Brennan et al., "Incidence of Adverse Events and Negligent Care in Hospitalized Patients," 321 *New England Journal of Medicine* 431 (1991); Lucian L. Leape et al., "The Nature of Adverse Events in Hospitalized Patients," 321 *New England Journal of Medicine* 438 (1991); Troyen A. Brennan et al., "Hospital Characteristics Associated with Adverse Events and Negligent Care," 265 *Journal of the American Medical Association* 3265 (1991).

17. Nor can one find the explanation for such high rates of iatrogenic injuries in limitations placed on the care at the choice of the individual patient. Any voluntary decisions regarding limitation in care were noted in our review, and we found very few "Do Not Resuscitate" (DNR) or other such orders.

18. An analysis of adverse event rates among patients over 45 years of age revealed that patients with Medicare had higher adverse event rates (6.5 percent) than privately insured patients (4.9 percent) ($p = .003$), but this may have been

due to age confounding (most Medicare patients are over 65 and so at greater risk for negligent care).

19. Diagnosis Related Groups are classifications of care based on diagnosis and therapy. For example, one DRG concerns surgical treatment of gall bladder disease. DRGs were developed as a means for comparing hospitals, especially for compensation purposes. The federal government now uses DRGs to compensate hospitals for care on a prospective basis. Each discharge from a hospital is assigned a primary DRG, and this governs the amount the hospital will be compensated for the particular case. See Bruce C. Vladeck, "Medicare Hospital Payment by Diagnosis Related Groups," 100 *Annals of Internal Medicine* 576 (1984).

20. Actually, we grouped all the DRGs into four risk categories, ranked according to the DRG's propensity to give rise to an adverse event. For details, see Brennan et al., "Hospital Characteristics."

21. These findings of increased negligence for the aged and the uninsured persist through various specifications of the logistic regression model. Since high correlations are found between black race, uninsured status, hospital minority discharges, and hospital self-pay/Medicaid discharges, we sequentially removed each variable from the model to avoid highly linked associations. If black race is removed from the model, the risk of negligence for the uninsured increases to 2.2 (p = .04). When the hospital-level factors of percentage of minority discharges and the percentage of self-pay/Medicaid discharges are sequentially removed from the model, self-pay at the patient level remains a significant risk factor for negligence (p = .03). When all hospital characteristics are removed from the model, the uninsured (odds ratio = 2.5, p = .007) and the aged (OR = 1.96, p = .02) remain at increased risk for substandard care. (Moreover, when payor status is completely removed from the model, no individual or hospital factors are associated with substandard care.)

22. See Harvard Study, pp. 18–20.

23. For the estimated 6,000 workplace fatalities every year, see U.S. Office of Technology Assessment, *Preventing Illness and Injury in the Workplace* 30–31 (Washington, D.C.: U.S. Government Printing Office, 1985). For the estimated 50,000 motor vehicle fatalities, see National Safety Council, *Accident Facts* (Chicago, 1988), pp. 3, 59.

24. For example, Yergan and colleagues found that nonwhite patients with pneumonia received fewer hospital services than expected on the basis of medical problems; see Daniel Yergan et al., "Relationship between Patient Race and the Intensity of Hospital Services," 25 *Medical Care* 592 (1987). Bombardier and colleagues studied 11 noncardiac surgical procedures and found that whites underwent significantly more procedures than blacks; see Claire Bombardier et al., "Socioeconomic Factors Affecting the Utilization of Surgical Operations," 297 *New England Journal of Medicine* 699 (1977). When these investigators controlled for income, however, the interracial differences became smaller and were no

longer statistically significant. Recently Wenneker and Epstein found less coronary angiography, coronary artery bypass grafting operations, and coronary angioplasty among blacks; see Mark Wenneker and Arnold Epstein, "Racial Inequalities in the Use of Procedures for Patients with Ischemic Heart Disease in Massachussetts," 261 *Journal of the American Medical Association* 253 (1989). Of course, less utilization of resources does not necessarily mean that blacks receive poorer medical care. However, a series of studies has demonstrated that neonatal mortality is higher among black children at all income levels; see, e.g., Paul H. Wise et al., "Racial and Socioeconomic Disparities in Childhood Mortality in Boston," 313 *New England Journal of Medicine* 360 (1985); Edward J. Lammer et al., "Classification and Analysis of Fetal Deaths in Massachusetts," 261 *Journal of the American Medical Association* 1757 (1989). Moreover, it appears that nonwhite patients have only half as much chance of receiving a renal transplant as do white patients of the same age and sex; see Carl M. Kjellstrand, "Age, Sex, and Race Inequality in Renal Transplant," 148 *Archives of Internal Medicine* 1305 (1988).

25. This is especially true of screening for chronic diseases; see Steffie Woolhandler and David Himmelstein, "Reverse Targeting of Preventive Care Due to Lack of Health Insurance," 259 *Journal of the American Medical Association* 2872 (1988). One study showed that termination from MediCal (the California Medicaid Program) led to significantly worse control of high blood pressure and diabetes among patients; see Nicole Lurie et al., "Termination from MediCal: Does It Affect Health?" 311 *New England Journal of Medicine* 480 (1984). Another study found significant increases in poor outcomes among pregnant women without insurance; see Paula Braveman et al., "Lack of Health Insurance and Adverse Outcomes in Newborns in an Eight-County Area of California, 1982–1986," 321 *New England Journal of Medicine* 508 (1989).

26. See Troyen A. Brennan, *Just Doctoring: Medical Ethics in the Liberal State* (Berkeley: University of California Press, 1991).

27. See Leon Wyszewianski, "Quality of Care: Past Achievements and Future Challenges," 25 *Inquiry* 13 (1988); Katherine N. Lohr et al., "Current Issues in Quality of Care," 7 *Health Affairs* 5 (1988).

28. A number of researchers have tried to relate hospital attributes to better care. See Joel S. Feigenson et al., "Outcome and Cost for Stroke Patients in Academic and Community Hospitals: A Comparison of Two Groups Referred to a Regional Rehabilitation Center," 240 *Journal of the American Medical Association* 1878–80 (1978); Stephen M. Shortell et al., "Hospital Medical Staff Organization and Quality of Care: Results for Myocardial Infarction and Appendectomy," 19 *Medical Care* 1041 (1981).

29. See Judy Ann Bigby et al., "Assessing the Preventability of Emergency Hospital Admission," 83 *American Journal of Medicine* 1031 (1986); Charles Safran et al., "Interventions to Prevent Readmission: The Constraints of Cost and Efficacy," 27 *Medical Care* 204 (1989).

30. See Robert W. Dubois et al., "Adjusted Hospital Death Rates: A Potential Screen for Quality of Medical Care," 77 *American Journal of Public Health* 1162 (1987).

31. Arthur J. Hartz et al., "Hospital Characteristics and Mortality Rates," 321 *New England Journal of Medicine* 1720 (1989).

32. Arlene Fink et al., "The Condition of the Literature on Differences in Hospital Mortality," 27 *Medical Care* 315 (1989).

33. Jesse Green et al., "The Importance of Severity of Illness in Assessing Hospital Mortality," 263 *Journal of the American Medical Association* 241 (1990); and David W. Smith, "Using Clinical Variables to Estimate the Risk of Patient Mortality," 29 *Medical Care* 1108 (1991).

34. Rolla E. Park et al., "Explaining Variations in Hospital Death Rates: Randomness, Severity of Illness, and Quality of Care," 264 *Journal of the American Medical Association* 484 (1990).

35. Donald M. Berwick et al., "Hospital Leaders' Opinions of the HCFA Mortality Data," 263 *Journal of the American Medical Association* 247 (1990).

36. Kathrine L. Kahn et al., "The Effects of the DRG-Based Prospective Payment System on Quality of Care for Hospitalized Patients: An Introduction to the Series," 264 *Journal of the American Medical Association* 1953 (1990).

37. See Mark Grady, "Why Are People Negligent? Technology, Nondurable Precautions, and the Medical Malpractice Explosion," 52 *Northwestern University Law Review* 293 (1988). The most recently heralded illustration of this phenomenon is the development of new techniques for operating on the fetus while it is still in the mother's womb in order to remove serious congenital defects.

4. Patient Injury and Malpractice Litigation

1. See Richard L. Abel, "The Real Tort Crisis—Too Few Claims," 48 *Ohio State Law Journal* 443, 448 (1987).

2. Patricia M. Danzon, *Medical Malpractice: Theory, Evidence, and Public Policy* 22–25 (Cambridge, Mass.: Harvard University Press, 1985). See William B. Schwartz and Neil K. Komesar, "Doctors, Damages, and Deterrence: An Economic View of Malpractice," 298 *New England Journal of Medicine* 1282 (1978), for an earlier analysis along the same lines.

3. California Medical Association, *Medical Insurance Feasibility Study*, ed. Donald H. Mills (San Francisco: Sutter Publications, 1977).

4. Patricia M. Danzon, "Medical Malpractice Liability," in Robert E. Litan and Clifford Winston, eds., *Liability: Perspectives and Policy* 101, 117 (Washington, D.C.: Brookings Institution, 1988).

5. U.S. General Accounting Office (GAO), *Medical Malpractice: Six State Case Studies* 17 (Washington, D.C.: U.S. Government Printing Office, 1986).

6. 1975 New York Laws, Ch. 109, § 2. Subsequent amendments required reporting from hospitals that were self-insured or insured by out-of-state carriers;

see 1978 New York Laws, Ch. 141, § 1; 1980 New York Laws, Ch. 866, § 17; New York Laws, Ch. 357, § 1. In addition, on June 30, 1988, the New York legislature passed an amendment to clarify the obligation of all hospitals not insured by a conventional insurer to report suits and requests for payment to the Department of Health; see 1988 New York Laws, Ch. 184, § 6 (McKinney) (Amending New York Insurance Law, § 315 (b) ((2)).

7. A recent RAND study, Deborah R. Hensler et al., *Compensation for Accidental Injuries in the United States* (Santa Monica, Calif.: RAND Institute for Civil Justice, 1991), surveyed a nationwide sample of families to determine the incidence, causes, and reactions to accidental injuries. Only 1 percent of total reported injuries (p. 31) were attributed by the respondents to medical treatment (and more than half of these to drug reactions). This is a far smaller medical share of the accident total one obtains by comparing the populationwide estimates of medical injuries based on the New York and California direct reviews of hospital records with reported motor vehicle and occupational accident rates.

8. GAO, *Medical Malpractice: Six State Case Studies,* p. 17.

9. Report of the New York State Insurance Department on Medical Malpractice, *A Balanced Prescription for Change* 58 (Albany, 1988).

10. This matching procedure is described in detail in Harvard Study, technical appendix 7.V.1.

11. See Harvard Study, pp. 7:13–24.

12. GAO, *Medical Malpractice: Six State Case Studies,* p. 17.

13. And these calculations make the unrealistic assumption that all presently paid claims involve patients with serious rather than modest injuries. If one assumed, for example, that one-third of the successful claims were for relatively short-lived injuries or to patients who were more than 70 years old, the ratio of serious physical and financial injury to tort claim would be approximately 3 to 1. And if one excludes only the modestly disabled from the calculations, the gap doubles between serious negligent injury suffered by young and old patients and malpractice claims made and paid.

14. For further details, see A. Russell Localio, Ann G. Lawthers, Troyen A. Brennan, et al., "Findings from the Harvard Medical Practice Study, III," 325 *New England Journal of Medicine* 245 (1991).

15. Frederick W. Cheney, Karen Posner, Robert A. Caplan, and Richard J. Ward, "Standard of Care and Anesthesia Liability," 261 *Journal of the American Medical Association* 1599 (1989).

16. Henry S. Farber and Michelle J. White, "Medical Malpractice: An Empirical Examination of the Litigation Process," 22 *RAND Journal of Economics* 199 (1990).

17. The observation in the text is accurate only if one considers (as did the two studies referred to) the disposition of all malpractice claims, whether this occurs through withdrawal, settlement, or trial. Only about 10 percent of malpractice claims produce a jury verdict, of which patients tend to win roughly a

third (sharply lower than the plaintiff success rate in other types of personal injury litigation). The one study we have of the merits of jury verdicts in malpractice cases, Thomas B. Metzloff, "Resolving Malpractice Disputes: Imaging the Jury's Shadow," 54 *Law and Contemporary Problems* 43 (1991), found that North Carolina patient-claimants from 1984 to 1987 won jury victories in only about half the cases that the malpractice insurers themselves had adjudged to be probably meritorious.

18. One should not assume, however, that a patient's filing of an invalid malpractice claim is as irrational and arbitrary an act as the police officer's ticketing of a driver for going through a green light. Through the patient survey described in the next chapter, we interviewed all injured patients (and a matched control group of noninjured patients) about their subsequent financial losses. For the reasons stated in the text, we could make contact with only a tiny number of patients (15) who had filed tort claims. But using their experience as something of a comparative benchmark, we found that the tort claimants had, on average, suffered far higher post-hospitalization losses than the overall (injured) patient population. For example, the injured worker claimants suffered wage losses approximately three times as great as did all injured workers and were reimbursed through disability insurance for a much smaller proportion of these much higher wage losses. One would surmise, then, that it is this huge compensation gap that sends patients to lawyers seeking redress for their needs that is not available from other sources. We shall address later the policy implications of that natural human reaction.

19. See, for example, Jean A. Macchiaroli, "Medical Malpractice Screening Panels: Proposed Model Legislation to Cure Judicial Ills," 58 *George Washington Law Review* 181 (1990).

20. See Patricia Munch Danzon and Lee A. Lillard, "Settlement out of Court: The Disposition of Medical Malpractice Claims," 12 *Journal of Legal Studies* 345, 373–374 (1983); and Stephen Shmanske and Tina Stevens, "The Performance of Medical Malpractice Review Panels," 11 *Journal of Health Politics, Policy, and Law* 525 (1986).

21. Or who, having sued, fail to persuade a jury of the merits of their case: see Metzloff, "Resolving Malpractice Disputes."

5. Patient Losses and Compensation

1. See Ernest J. Weinrib, "Understanding Tort Law," 23 *Valparaiso University Law Review* 485 (1989).

2. The following are the more notable pieces of research about the losses suffered and compensation received by the victims of specific categories of injuries: U.S. Department of Transportation, *Economic Consequences of Automobile Accident Injuries* (Washington, D.C.: U.S. Government Printing Office, 1970) (1969 survey of a nationwide sample of 1,037 victims of at least moderately

serious motor vehicle injuries); William G. Johnson, Paul R. Cullinan, and William Curington, "The Adequacy of Workers' Compensation Benefits," in 5 *Research Report of the U.S. Interdepartmental Workers' Compensation Task Force* 95– 120 (Washington, D.C.: U.S. Government Printing Office, 1979) (1976 survey of 1,918 workers in five states who had been permanently injured in an occupational accident in the years 1968–1970, and whose economic situation through 1975 was investigated); William G. Johnson and Edward Heler, "The Costs of Asbestos-Associated Disease and Death," 61 *Milbank Memorial Fund Quarterly: Health and Society* 177–194 (Spring 1983); and William G. Johnson and Edward Heler, "Compensation for Death from Asbestos," 37 *Industrial and Labor Relations Review* 529–540 (1984) (1980 survey of 560 widows of men who had died in the years 1967–1976 as a result of an asbestos-related disease, to determine the economic situation of the widows up through 1979); James K. Hammitt et al., *Automobile Accident Compensation* (Santa Monica, Calif.: RAND Institute for Civil Justice, 1985) (in particular, its 1977 survey of nearly 1,500 households that had experienced an injury in a motor vehicle accident in the years 1975–1977, and who were interviewed about their experience during the most recent period of temporary disability); and James S. Kakalik et al., *Aviation Accident Study* (Santa Monica, Calif.: RAND Institute for Civil Justice, 1988) (a survey of the survivors of all 2,198 victims of every major airline crash in the United States from 1970 through 1984, to determine all the net financial losses experienced or predicted for these survivors, and all the tort compensation they received). In addition to the above, two major national surveys have been conducted of the experience of injury victims from all causes. The Oxford study in Great Britain is reported in Donald Harris et al., *Compensation and Support for Illness and Injury* (Oxford: Clarendon Press, 1984); and the RAND study for the United States is reported in Deborah R. Hensler et al., *Compensation for Accidental Injuries in the United States* (Santa Monica, Calif.: RAND Institute for Civil Justice, 1991). Finally, a still more recent study, Frank A. Sloan and Stephen S. Van Wert, "Costs and Compensation of Injuries in Medical Malpractice," 54 *Law and Contemporary Problems* 131 (1991), interviewed a number of Florida patients who had filed malpractice claims in the 1980s, to determine the extent of economic losses and the amount of compensation received through tort litigation (though not from other insurance sources).

3. To give some sense of the relative role of tort litigation as a source of compensation for injury victims, Jeffrey O'Connell and James Guinivan, "An Irrational Combination: Relative Expansion of Liability Insurance and Contraction of Loss Insurance," 49 *Ohio State Law Journal* 757 (1988), estimate that the tort contribution in 1984 (just under $40 billion) was only one-tenth the total paid by loss insurance programs.

4. See the calculations by Patricia Danzon in Henry G. Manne, ed., *Medical Malpractice Policy Guidebook* 128–142 (Jacksonville: Florida Medical Association, 1985). To the same effect for product liability, see W. Kip Viscusi, "Pain and

Suffering in Product Liability Cases: Systematic Compensation or Capricious Awards?" 8 *International Review of Law and Economics* 203 (1988).

5. For a review of the issues and the literature, see Paul C. Weiler, *Medical Malpractice on Trial* 54–61 (Cambridge, Mass.: Harvard University Press, 1991).

6. See ibid., pp. 31–32, 50–54.

7. See the discussion and references in ibid., pp. 53, 139–140.

8. For comparative descriptions of the systems in these two countries, see Marilynn M. Rosenthal, *Dealing with Medical Malpractice: The British and Swedish Experience* (Durham, N.C.: Duke University Press, 1988); and Walter Gellhorn, "Medical Malpractice Litigation (U.S.)—Medical Mishap Compensation (N.Z.)," 73 *Cornell Law Review* 170 (1988).

9. For a detailed description of the patient survey instrument and methodology, see Harvard Study, chap. 8 and technical appendixes.

10. See ibid., pp. 8:47–50 and table 8.1.

11. Subsequent in-depth analysis of potential nonresponse bias in the interview survey demonstrates that this factor did not affect the results for medical care costs, at least; see Sybil Crawford, William G. Johnson, and Nan Laird, "Bayes Analysis for Model Based Methods for Non-Ignorable Non-Response in Sample Surveys" (Harvard School of Public Health, 1991).

12. See James Lambrinos, "On the Use of Historical Data in the Estimation of Economic Losses," 52 *Journal of Risk and Insurance* 464 (1988) (updated to 1990 in personal communication with author).

13. Men on average spend roughly one-quarter as much time on household production as do married women; see Kathryn E. Walker and Margaret E. Woods, *Time Use: A Measure of Household Production of Family Goods and Services* (Washington, D.C.: American Home Economics Association, 1976).

14. Walker and Woods, *Time Use.*

15. U.S. Department of Labor, Bureau of Labor Statistics, *Revised Equivalence Scales for Estimating Equivalent Incomes or Budget Costs by Family Type* (Washington, D.C.: U.S. Government Printing Office, 1968).

16. Thus, since we excluded from our estimates any losses that occurred in the first six months from the date of hospitalization, we also excluded any offsetting compensation benefits received during that period.

17. See Martin Feldstein and Lawrence Summers, "Inflation, Tax Rules, and Long-term Interest Rates," *Brookings Papers on Economic Activity* 1 (1978).

18. To take one example, an individual with severe diabetes may develop peripheral disease of the artery and veins. This vascular impairment can necessitate amputation of part of the patient's extremities. In evaluation for such surgery, the person undergoes radiological procedures to determine the extent of this disease. These radiological tests require insertion of a contrast dye into the patient's veins. In a particular case the dye caused a kidney failure, i.e., an adverse event. However, the transient disability from this renal failure, though identifiable as a separate harm from the underlying vascular disease, in fact

contributed only a small portion of the subsequent disability experienced by the patient.

19. See Harvard Study, technical appendix 8.IV.1, for the details of the physician attribution procedure.

20. For details of the selection of the control group, see ibid., technical appendix 8.IV.2.

21. This method has been widely utilized in analysis of wage differentials between men and women and white and black workers; see, e.g., Ronald S. Oaxaca, "Male-Female Wage Differentials in Urban Labor Markets," 14 *International Economic Review* 693 (October 1973); and Alan S. Blinder, "Wage Discrimination: Reduced Form and Structural Estimates," 8 *Journal of Human Resources* 463 (1973).

22. This estimate was derived as follows. In 1988, the latest year for which figures were available, the state's Insurance Department reported that doctors and hospitals paid approximately $850 million in direct malpractice premiums. Our analysis of data from 1984 (when direct premiums were slightly under $300 million) indicated that an additional 40 percent or more in malpractice costs were incurred by various health care organizations on self-insurance against medical liability. Although it is unlikely that self-insurance costs jumped as much after 1984 as did direct premiums paid, the estimate in the text of more than $1 billion for total malpractice costs in the state is quite conservative.

23. See Weiler, *Medical Malpractice on Trial*, p. 53.

24. See George L. Priest, "The Current Insurance Crisis in Modern Tort Law," 96 *Yale Law Journal* 1521, 1560 (1987).

25. Weiler, *Medical Malpractice on Trial*, pp. 47–61, 134–139.

26. See Randall R. Bovbjerg, Frank A. Sloan, and James F. Blumstein, "Valuing Life and Limb in Tort: Scheduling 'Pain and Suffering,'" 83 *Northwestern University Law Review* 908 (1989); and Monroe Berkowitz and John F. Burton, *Permanent Disability Benefits in Workers' Compensation* (Kalamazoo, Mich.: W. E. Upjohn Institute for Employment, 1987).

27. The federal government has adopted regulations that make Medicare and Medicaid the second payor to third-party liability systems, and these federal rules preempt contrary state laws regarding no-fault auto liability; see Abrams v. Heckler, 582 F.Supp. 1155 (S.D.N.Y. 1984); and Rubin v. Sullivan, 720 F.Supp. 840 (D.C. Hawaii, 1989). Federal insistence on that policy in this context would pose a special problem for no-fault patient compensation, because many of the most difficult causation problems we encountered involved the elderly, for whom the key compensable losses primarily involved medical care. Thus, significant administrative costs would have to be expended just to determine which government-initiated insurance program would cover these medical expenses. We are confident (as is the government of New York) that if no-fault patient compensation is considered a sensible program on its merits, special exemption can be secured from these federal regulations (since, unlike the case

with motor vehicle accidents, Medicare and Medicaid expenditures now cover the liability insurance costs of medical injuries to their constituents, whether the basis of liability be tort-fault or no-fault). Thus we made our basic calculations on the assumption that the second-payor status of no-fault patient compensation would apply to Medicare and Medicaid. However, we also provide an estimate in the text of how much in additional expenditures would ride on this item.

6. Malpractice Litigation and Injury Prevention

1. The most prominent exponent of this persuasion within medical liability is Patricia M. Danzon; see her *Medical Malpractice: Theory, Evidence, and Public Policy* (Cambridge, Mass.: Harvard University Press, 1985).

2. A substantial preventive value from no-fault workers' compensation has been demonstrated by Professors Michael J. Moore and W. Kip Viscusi; see their *Compensation Mechanisms for Job Risks: Wages, Workers' Compensation, and Product Liability* 121–135 (Princeton: Princeton University Press, 1990) and "Promoting Safety through Workers' Compensation: The Efficacy and Net Wage Costs of Injury Insurance," 20 *RAND Journal of Economics* 499 (1989), which estimate that existing workers' compensation programs in the United States can be credited with reducing by anywhere from 25 to 45 percent (depending on the statistical methodology utilized) the number of fatalities that would otherwise have occurred in American workplaces.

3. On the latter point, see Danzon, *Medical Malpractice*, pp. 139–143.

4. Compare Peter A. Bell, "Legislative Intrusions into the Common Law of Medical Malpractice: Thoughts about the Deterrent Effect of Tort Liability," 35 *Syracuse Law Review* 939 (1984), with Howard A. Latin, "Problem-Solving Behavior and Theories of Tort Liability," 73 *California Law Review* 677 (1985).

5. See John E. Rolph, "Some Statistical Evidence on Merit Rating in Medical Malpractice Insurance," 48 *Journal of Risk and Insurance* 247 (1981); and Frank A. Sloan, Randall Bovbjerg, and Penny Githens, *Insuring Medical Malpractice* (New York: Oxford University Press, 1991).

6. As good an index as any of the felt consequences of malpractice litigation is the intensity with which physician associations have pursued statutory restraints on litigation through the state legislatures.

7. Actually there have been two excellent empirical studies of the impact of appelate court decisions upon physician behavior: the first by Jerry Wiley, "The Impact of Judicial Decisions on Professional Conduct: An Empirical Study," 55 *Southern California Law Review* 345 (1981) (finding no influence of the *Helling* decision, which held ophthalmologists negligent for failing to do routine glaucoma testing on even their younger patients); the second by Daniel J. Givelber, William J. Bowers, and Carolyn L. Blitch, "*Tarasoff*, Myth and Reality: An Empirical Study of Private Law in Action," 1984 *Wisconsin Law Review* 443 (finding some influence from the *Tarasoff* decision, holding psychiatrists negligent

for failing to warn a potential victim of the threat of violence by a patient under therapy). But while such influence of judicial rulings upon physician behavior is a necessary precondition for a preventive impact of malpractice law, it is not a sufficient condition. One must also be able to detect a reduction in patient injuries from this altered mode of medical practice. By analogy, it has been shown that employers are moved by Occupational Safety and Health Administration (OSHA) standards to undertake major capital expenditures to try to make their workplaces safer (see, e.g., Ann P. Bartel and Lucy Glenn Thomas, "Direct and Indirect Effects of Regulation," 28 *Journal of Law and Economics* 10 [1985]), but researchers have discerned only a modest impact of such OSHA efforts on the bottom-line incidence of occupational injuries (see W. Kip Viscusi, "The Impact of Occupational Safety and Health Regulation, 1973–83," 17 *RAND Journal of Economics* 567 [1983]; and Leon S. Robertson and J. Phillip Keeve, "Worker Injuries: The Effect of Workers' Compensation and OSHA Inspections," 8 *Journal of Health Politics, Policy, and Law* 581 [1983]).

8. The best review of this growing body of empirical research is by Donald Dewees and Michael Trebilcock, *The Efficacy of the Tort System: A Review of the Empirical Evidence* II:20–34 (Philadelphia: American Law Institute, 1989). Among the key studies reviewed are Elizabeth Landes, "Insurance, Liability, and Accidents: A Theoretical and Empirical Investigation of the Effect of No-Fault Accidents," 25 *Journal of Law and Economics* 49 (1982) (finding that no-fault does increase motor vehicle fatalities); and Paul Zader and Adrian Lund, "Re-Analysis of the Effect of No-Fault Auto Insurance on Fatal Crashes," 55 *Journal of Risk and Insurance* 236 (1986) (finding no such increase).

9. The first study, by Marc Gaudry, "The Effect on Road Safety of the Compulsory Insurance, Flat Premium Rating, and No-Fault Features of the 1978 Quebec Automobile Act," in 2 *Report of Inquiry into Motor Vehicle Accident Compensation in Ontario* 1–28 (Toronto: Queen's Printer for Ontario, 1988), found a 7 percent increase in automobile fatalities, all of which was accounted for by the new flat-rate pricing system in Quebec's no-fault program, a feature that apparently attracted onto the province's highways larger numbers of high-risk drivers. The second study, by Rose-Ann Devlin, "Liability versus No-Fault Automobile Insurance Regimes: An Analysis of the Experience in Quebec" (Ph.D. diss., University of Toronto, 1988), found a 14 percent increase in driving fatalities, some of which was attributed to a reduction in actual driving precautions induced by no-fault.

10. The last decision posed the problem of how to treat claims made against physicians who had staff privileges at more than one hospital. In fact we had no choice but to count a claim against any such physician as part of the total for each of the hospitals with which that physician was affiliated. The reason is that the data available to us did not link claims against a physician to the particular hospital in which the treatment had occurred. The method we used—counting such claims against all the hospital groups within which the physician

practiced—seemed to accord with the theory of general deterrence underlying tort law, which assumes that other doctors will be aware of and influenced by the experience of litigation against one of their medical colleagues. That should be so irrespective of whether the claim happened to arise from treatment delivered at one hospital rather than another. To the extent that this assumption was incorrect, and the deterrent effect of any one claim was felt only among the doctors in the hospital in which the treatment occurred, our inability to make the claims threat precise in that manner introduced some random measurement error into the claims variable: the effect was to reduce rather than to enhance our ability to detect a preventive impact from this legal deterrent factor.

The claims numbers and rates used in this econometric analysis are considerably higher than those used in the litigation analysis in Chapter 4. There are two major reasons for this. One is that we counted separately here all the claims brought by a patient against any provider (both the hospital and one or more doctors) that arose out of the same incident. The other reason is that we counted any claim against a physician with multiple hospital affiliations as part of the total assigned to each hospital grouping.

11. We could not dismiss this issue on the ground that our claims variable was for the year 1983 and our injury variable was for 1984, and simply assert that negligent hospital injuries in 1984 could not have produced malpractice claims in 1983. The reason is that the claims distribution across hospitals was quite stable over time. Thus, if there were some accident-prone physicians practicing in one hospital throughout the 1980s, the high claims rate against that hospital group in 1983 would be an effect of the same pattern of behavior we observed in the 1984 hospital charts.

12. In our initial work, we simply used the rate of claims per hospital admission. This technique ignored the problem of reciprocal causation discussed in the text and produced results that were inconclusive, both in point estimate and in statistical significance; see Harvard Study, pp. 10:39–48.

13. At many of the hospitals there were small numbers of negligent events in our sample, which meant the observed rates of claims per negligent event would not necessarily be good estimates of rates that would be observed in a larger sample. The problem is analogous to estimating a baseball player's end-of-season batting average after only a few at bats. For that reason, we "smoothed" the values of claims per negligent adverse event. At large hospitals the rate we used differs little from the value we observed in the sample, but at smaller hospitals the value is closer to the mean value across all hospitals. We also weighted the observations in proportion to the weight of the case, as described in Chapter 3.

14. See G. S. Maddala, *Limited Dependent and Qualitative Variables in Econometrics* (New York: Cambridge University Press, 1983).

15. Previous research has shown that urbanization is a very powerful external predictor of malpractice claims. See Danzon, *Medical Malpractice*, pp. 74–75. (Indeed, after this factor is controlled for, the number of lawyers per capita

has no effect on claiming propensity.) Because urban areas are more likely to have a higher population density, we consider that such higher density might itself be an independent predictor of claims.

16. In addition, we ran two statistical tests of our assumption that these instrumental variables were not directly related to medical injury rates; each of the variables passed these tests.

17. For a considerable period the estimates we derived from the model described earlier did reach the level of statistical significance. We were concerned, though, about the reliability of the precise technique that was then available to us for calculating the confidence intervals. When we finally were able to devise a more satisfactory methodology for that purpose, we were disappointed to learn that our point estimates (which were still approximately the same in size) no longer passed this key scientific test.

18. See Danzon, *Medical Malpractice,* p. 226.

7. Ruminations for the Future

1. See the capsule summary and references in Paul C. Weiler, *Medical Malpractice on Trial* (Cambridge, Mass.: Harvard University Press, 1991), chap. 2.

2. Report of the American Medical Association/Specialty Society Medical Liability Project, *A Proposed Alternative to the Civil Justice System for Resolving Medical Liability Disputes: A Fault-Based Administrative System* (Chicago: AMA, 1987).

3. See Randall R. Bovbjerg and Clark C. Havighurst, eds., "Symposium: Medical Malpractice: Can the Private Sector Find Relief?" 49 *Law and Contemporary Problems* 1 (1986).

4. See Randall R. Bovbjerg, Laurence R. Tancredi, and Daniel S. Gaylin, "Obstetrics and Malpractice: Evidence on the Performance of a Selective No-Fault System," 265 *Journal of the American Medical Association* 2836 (1991).

5. California Medical Association, *Medical Insurance Feasibility Study,* ed. Donald H. Mills (San Francisco: Sutter Publications, 1977).

6. See Henry S. Farber and Michelle J. White, "Medical Malpractice: An Empirical Examination of the Litigation Process," 22 *RAND Journal of Economics* 199 (1991); and Frederick W. Cheney, Karen Posner, Robert A. Caplan, and Richard J. Ward, "Standard of Care and Anesthesia Liability," 261 *Journal of the American Medical Association* 1599 (1989). Compare, however, Thomas B. Metzloff, "Resolving Malpractice Disputes: Imaging the Jury's Shadow," 54 *Law and Contemporary Problems* 43 (1991), on the somewhat less accurate performance of the jury system in the 10 percent or so of total malpractice claims that do get to trial.

7. And as we noted in Chapter 4, one apparent reason why patients who have not suffered negligent injuries go to a lawyer in the first place is that they experienced much greater uncompensated losses as an offshoot of their hospitalization.

8. A recent study, Deborah R. Hensler et al., *Compensation of Accidental Injuries in the United States* (Santa Monica, Calif.: RAND Institute of Civil Justice, 1991), shows that this phenomenon is equally, if not more, visible outside the medical arena. For example, of respondents in a national survey who reported a *serious* injury from a consumer product, just 20 percent even considered filing a claim, 7 percent took some action, 5 percent consulted a lawyer, and 3 percent hired a lawyer (p. 127). And as is generally true in the tort system, hiring a lawyer by no means guarantees recovery of any damages, let alone full redress.

9. As to the latter, see Barry Manuel, "Professional Liability—A No-Fault Alternative," 322 *New England Journal of Medicine* 627 (1990).

10. In particular, in Weiler, *Medical Malpractice on Trial.*

11. For more extensive elaboration of this argument see ibid., chap. 6.

12. See Michael J. Moore and W. Kip Viscusi, *Compensation Mechanisms for Job Risks: Wages, Workers' Compensation, and Product Liability* 121–135 (Princeton: Princeton University Press, 1990).

13. See John H. Eichhorn, Jeffrey B. Cooper, David J. Cullen, et al., "Standards for Patient Monitoring during Anesthesia at Harvard Medical School," 256 *Journal of the American Medical Association* 1017 (1986).

14. The principal focus of this book has been on alternative ways in which judges and lawyers can deploy the resources of the law to motivate health care providers to avoid injury to patients. We have not tried to map paths that might be followed by professionals inside the health care system toward safer and more effective medical care. However, our proposed shift in the focus of legal liability from the personal fault of individual doctor to the collective responsibility of the health care organization has a clear affinity with a new systems-based approach to quality management now emerging within the American health care system.

Just like malpractice litigation, the health care system has traditionally treated quality issues as the responsibility of autonomous physicians, policed only by highly stylized forms of peer evaluation in hospital "morbidity and mortality conferences" (see Troyen Brennan, *Just Doctoring: Medical Ethics in the Liberal State* 123 [Berkeley: University of California Press, 1991]). Over the last twenty years, though, there has occurred a pronounced shift in the balance of power within the hospital from physician to central administration, largely propelled by the pressures of complex reimbursement and cost containment programs in contemporary health care financing (see Rosemary Stevens, *In Sickness and in Wealth: American Hospitals in the Twentieth Century* 341–344 [New York: Basic Books, 1989]). Unsurprisingly, then, as malpractice liability costs have soared, hospital administrators have established risk management programs as well.

To the extent that "risk management" means not simply reducing the odds of successful suit by patients who happened to be injured, but reducing the odds of medical injury in the first place, such an institutional emphasis on quality assurance seems to us the most promising avenue toward safer care. We have in mind, particularly, the notion of "total quality management," which seeks to adapt to the health care setting the most sophisticated forms of product quality management developed in modern industry (see Donald M. Berwick, "Continuous Improvement as an Ideal in Health Care," 320 *New England Journal of Medicine* 53 [1989]; and Glenn Laffell and David Blumenthal, "The Case for Using Industrial Quality Management Science in Health Care Organizations," 262 *Journal of the American Medical Association* 2859 [1989]).

15. See Weiler, *Medical Malpractice on Trial,* pp. 154–158.

16. For a more detailed presentation of this idea, see Reporters' Study, *Enterprise Responsibility for Personal Injury* (Philadelphia: American Law Institute, 1991), in particular vol. II, chap. 16 (authored by Paul Weiler, Chief Reporter for the ALI project).

17. These adjustments might well be made through direct agreement between the hospital and their medical staff about how to reallocate payments received by each for particular risky procedures, e.g., obstetrical deliveries.

18. For example, one can well imagine a program following the lead of a proposed bill in North Carolina, and deciding to finesse the extremely difficult task of attributing particular cases of cerebral palsy to obstetrical care provided years earlier by simply making all cerebral palsy cases eligible for specified types of benefits. (Presumably one would exclude cases involving genetic abnormality or maternal substance abuse, which are clearly unrelated to medical management.) See Julian D. Bobbitt, Maureen Kelly O'Connor, and H. Alexander Easley, "North Carolina's Proposed Birth-Related Neurological Impairment Act: A Provocative Alternative," 26 *Wake Forest Law Review* 837, 858–868 (1991).

Index